Recreations of an Anthologist

Recreations of an Anthologist

By
BRANDER MATTHEWS

Essay Index Reprint Series

BOOKS FOR LIBRARIES PRESS, INC.
FREEPORT, NEW YORK

First published 1904
Reprinted 1967

PS 2372
R4

LIBRARY OF CONGRESS CATALOG CARD NUMBER:

67-26766

PRINTED IN THE UNITED STATES OF AMERICA

CONTENTS

RECREATIONS OF AN ANTHOLOGIST

I

BY WAY OF INTRODUCTION

PRYING eyes all over the world are now seeking to spy out the secret motives of every human action and to find an explanation, more or less plausible, for all the freakish deeds and foolish misdeeds of mankind. But no one of these inquirers into the recesses of man's being has yet come forward with a wholly satisfactory explanation of the reasons which lead so many of us to find our chief pleasure in the seemingly idle pastime of "making a collection," as it is called. Why is it that many a man puts his whole heart in this gathering together of the objects of his seeking? There are not a few otherwise sensible beings, good citizens, voters, church-members, who act on the axiom that the chief end of man is to "make a collection,"—whether of books or of autographs, of fans or of playing cards, of postage-stamps or of pictorial posters, of coins or of counterfeit money.

Of course, there is no denying that any collection, a string of buttons or a shelfful of boot-heels has some scientific value; and more than once has the mere heaper up of unconsidered trifles rendered inestimable service to the avid investigator into the records of human endeavor. The acquisitive energy of the coin-collectors has led to the lighting up of many a dark spot in chronology; and the accumulative zeal of the autograph-collectors has preserved writings which have helped to elucidate many a doubtful point in history. Even a collection of the buttons of precocious poets or a gathering of the boot-heels of famous female authors might supply suggestive material to an inquisitive critic like Sainte-Beuve, who was forever striving to interpret the works of every writer by a painstaking analysis of all the petty facts of his or her personality.

But however much the collector may boast of the utility of his labors, he knows perfectly well that his motive is not utilitarian. If he is honest with himself, he will admit humbly that the attraction of "making a collection" does not lie in the ultimate value of the collection when it shall be completed (as far as that may be possible). In the immense majority of cases the beginnings of the collection were accidental and wholly devoid of purpose. Sometimes as the collection grew, the collector has become conscious of its possible importance to science; but the charm of collecting is wholly independent of the actual value of the things accumulated. Indeed, the collection seems to lose some of its interest the nearer it approaches to completion; and it is then increasingly in danger of being disposed of hastily by auction, by private sale or by donation to some museum, so that the former owner may be set free to start again on the joyful labor he delights in. The zest of the sport resides in the pursuit of the game, and not in the counting of the spoils of the chase. "To have and to hold" is not the collector's motto but "to seek and to find."

It is this accumulation that gives the collector his keenest pleasure, this adding together of specimen after specimen, with little thought as to the importance to any investigator of the material thus amassed. The collector is not conscious of any altruistic wish to help along some unknown scientific observer. On the contrary, it is for himself he is working; he is frankly selfish,—not to say greedy. He is on the alert for the objects of his desire, he is capturing them, storing them up one by one, setting them up over against each other, solely for his own enjoyment, to

4

satisfy some inner need of his own soul. And this is why the true collector is almost as likely to be miserly as he is to be liberal. Now and then there is a collector of books or of coins who is notorious for the pitiful delight he takes in denying all access to his treasures, over which he prefers to gloat in contemptible solitude. The spring which moves these meaner collectors is probably a primitive instinct for acquisition; it is a belated survival of an ancestral trait, useful enough, once upon a time, to that remote progenitor of ours who was Probably Arboreal and who needed to lay up stores of all sorts against the coming of winter. And in the pleasure the collector takes in arranging and in re-arranging the things he has brought together with an infinitude of effort, perhaps we ought to recognize a cropping-out of that other rudimentary instinct which is known as the play-impulse. But here, as elsewhere in the long story of the ascent of man, we can see a constant struggle upward. That which begins because of the brute instinct of acquisition, a wanton accumulation without regard to the value of the things heaped up or to the utility of the collection itself, is evolved in time into something higher; and those who begin by collecting buttons or boot-heels may develop at last into expert numismatists or learned archæologists. Thus it is, that civilized man, in "this so-called twentieth century" of ours, finds his profit in the survival of mere monkey-tricks inherited from that distant ancestor who hung suspended by his prehensile tail from the boughs of the forest primeval.

So far as I am aware no one has hitherto drawn attention to the obvious fact that the motives of the collector of buttons and of boot-heels are closely akin to those of the literary anthologists who gather into a single volume the scattered poems or prose specimens which seem to belong together. For his own idle amusement at first, he collects the poems of varied authorship which

deal with the same theme or which are written in the same form, considering in the one
case the divergency of treatment and in the
other the divergency of topic. He may be
a lover of the Nicotian weed, seeking out
all the ballads which have been indited in
praise of tobacco; or he may be a lover of
soulful verse, delighting in the variety of
the lyric as it flourished in English under
Elizabeth or under Victoria. And for his
own sole pleasure he begins by bringing
together the more accessible poems of the
type in which his interest has been awakened. Then he finds himself wondering
whether there are not many other poems of
this same type that he has failed to find;
and all at once he is launched on a voyage
of discovery from which he returns with
spoil of all sorts, and in the course of which
he makes acquaintance with many a far
country.

When he contemplates the treasures he
has thus been enabled to acquire as the
result of his diligent search, and more espe-

cially when he notes how much the charm
of certain of his old favorites has been en-
hanced by contrast with certain of his more
recent discoveries, then he is moved to share
his pleasure with others. He cannot help
feeling sure that what has given him so
much satisfaction is likely also to delight not
a few lovers of literature, whose attention
has not hitherto been attracted in that
special direction. So he pursues his search,
and he sets his collection in order, and he
seeks faithfully for the missing specimens;
and in time he publishes the result of his
gleanings. Thus it was that Bell was
inspired to present to the public his striking
selection from the beautiful songs which
besprinkle the works of the British dramatists. And thus it was that the present
writer has been moved to edit three several
anthologies as different in theme as may be.

'Poems of American Patriotism' was published in 1882 by Charles Scribner's Sons;
and it was reissued by the same firm in
1898, when it was included in a series of

reading-books for schools. 'Ballads of
Books' was published in 1886 by George
J. Coombes; and it served as the foundation for a volume of the same title prepared by Mr. Andrew Lang and published in London in 1888 by Longmans,
Green & Co. The original American
collection was reissued in New York in
1899 by Dodd, Mead & Co. 'American
Familiar Verse: *vers de société*' was published in 1904 by Longmans, Green &
Co. as a volume of the 'Wampum Library of American Literature.' A fourth
volume, planned long ago, and not yet
brought to completion, will select and set in
order the chief poems which deal with the
past history and which celebrate the present
beauty of New York.

The collection of the material for these
several volumes, the hunting up of the
poems which were not at hand, the sifting
out of the verses which were felt to be unworthy of their fellows, the preparation of
an authentic text and of proper introduc-

tory notes,—all this was a labor of love, no doubt, but it was a labor, for all that, a labor the weight of which no one will be disposed to deny who has ever ventured on the undertaking of an anthology. But it was a labor that of a certainty paid for itself in an increase of knowledge and in a broadening of outlook. And the search for the poems demanding inclusion in one or another of these three volumes led the writer into many a by-path of letters. It increased his liking for the curiosities of literature, as the elder Disraeli had termed them,—a liking originally awakened by a boyish perusal of Disraeli's own pages. To gratify this liking the papers in the present volume have been written.

They are, for the most part, minor anthologies, — collections not important enough or not bulking big enough to demand independent existence in a volume, each by itself. And some of them are fairly to be called by-products of the longer and more important collections. For example, the paper on the epigram as it has been written here in the United States was the natural result of the attempt to collect the best specimens of American familiar verse (*vers de société*), the lyrics which are brief and brilliant and buoyant. And the paper on the quatrain, as this has been handled by American lyrists, was the outgrowth of the collection of American epigrams which revealed the need of making clear the distinction between the epigram of the Greeks of old and the epigram of the English-speaking writers of to-day.

To most careless users of books the anthologist is but a compiler, like the lexicographer, "a harmless drudge;" yet if any anthologists were ever inclined toward boastfulness, they would have little difficulty in proving that the practitioners of their humble craft had deserved well of the republic of letters; and they might recall with satisfaction the fact that Longfellow had prepared a bulky tome of selections from the 'Poets and Poetry of Europe' and

that he had also supervised the long series of 'Poems of Places,' a lyrical gazeteer. They might well feel pride in claiming kinship in labor with the other American songster who has bestowed upon us 'A Victorian Anthology' and 'An American Anthology,' and with the British bard who made us all his debtors by the lyric jewels he heaped up in the 'Golden Treasury.'
(1904.)

II

A THEME, WITH VARIATIONS

THERE seems to be nothing that a small mind more eagerly delights in than the detection of the small resemblances which are likely to be discoverable when the works of different authors are rigorously compared; and there are assuredly few things that a large mind regards with a more languid interest than the foolish and futile accusations of plagiarism now and again bandied about in the public prints. The man of large mind is both tolerant and careless. He knows that it is not rare for the same thought to occur independently and almost simultaneously to two original thinkers—just as the suggestion of natural selection came to Darwin and Wallace almost at the same time. Moreover, he is well aware that all workers have a right to avail themselves of whatsoever has been accomplished by their predecessors, so long as they do not make false pretences or seek to gain credit under false colors.

If proof was needed that Poe was not a man of large mind, it might be found in the fact that he was guilty of an article on 'Mr. Longfellow and Other Plagiarists'; and no one was surprised to learn that Poe himself could be a plagiarist upon occasion, and that he borrowed for his 'Marginalia' Sheridan's joke about the phœnix and Mr. Whitbread's describing it as a poulterer would. Of course, it is possible that Poe invented this witticism for himself, although this is not at all likely, since the American lyrist was one of those who joked with difficulty. The jest, indeed, is very characteristic of the author of the 'School for Scandal'—and very unlike the other humorous attempts of the author of the 'Raven.'

Tennyson once wrote to a critic who had

pointed out certain parallelisms in the
'Princess': "Why not? Are not human
eyes all over the world looking at the same
objects, and must there not consequently be
coincidences of thought and impressions
and expressions? It is scarcely possible for
any one to say or write anything in this late
time of the world to which, in all the rest
of the literature of the world, a parallel
could not somewhere be found." Lowell
declared that it was now impossible to sink
a spade in the soil of Parnassus without dis-
turbing the bones of some dead poet.
Shelley went so far as to assert that "all
knowledge is reminiscence; the doctrine is
far more ancient than the times of Plato,
and as old as the venerable allegory that the
Muses are the daughters of Memory; not
one of the nine was ever said to be the child
of Invention." And Mr. Aldrich in his
quatrain on 'Originality' has asserted that

No bird has ever uttered note
That was not in some first bird's throat;
Since Eden's freshness and man's fall
No rose has been original.

Just as Poe probably borrowed his merry jest from Sheridan, so very likely the remark of one of the characters in 'Lady Windemere's Fan'—"I can resist everything—except temptation"—is perhaps a reminiscence of the saying of the medieval Franc-Archer de Bagnolet, quoted by Rabelais, "I am not afraid of anything—except danger." But it was apparently quite independently but almost simultaneously that a similar thought occurred to a Frenchman, an Englishman, and an American. The late Thomas B. Reed, sometime Speaker of the House of Representatives, once defined a statesman as "a successful politician—who is dead." Mr. Pinero, having in mind the rather boisterous humor of the 'Rivals' or of 'She Stoops to Conquer,' has asserted that "a comedy is often only a farce—by a deceased dramatist." And in the journal of the Goncourts we can read the kindred remark that "genius is the talent of a dead man."

A THEME, WITH VARIATIONS

When M. Rostand brought out 'L'Aiglon' its likeness in theme to 'Hamlet' was promptly pointed out; now the likeness of 'Hamlet' to the 'Oresteia' is a commonplace of scholarship; but there is no resemblance whatsoever between the French play and the Greek tragedy, although they have each of them a certain superficial similarity to the English drama. Here we see that two dramas, each of which resembles a third, are not necessarily like each other. Up to the present time no literary detective has accused Mark Twain of overt plagiarism because he — probably unconsciously — transplanted certain incidents of 'Romeo and Juliet' to the banks of the Mississippi, when Huckleberry Finn was setting before us boldly and simply the outcome of the long-standing Shepherdson-Grangerford feud. And, as yet, Mr. Kipling has not been held up to public contempt because he utilized in his story of the 'King's Ankus' certain devices which Chaucer had already employed in one of the 'Canterbury Tales.'

17

Mr. Kipling's 'Brushwood Boy' is one of the most beautiful of his stories, and it is one of the most original, both in conception and execution. But at the core of it is the possibility of two persons meeting in their dreams; and this idea was already to be found in Mr. Du Maurier's 'Peter Ibbetson.' The same idea has since been developed by Mr. Marion Crawford in 'Cecilia;' and also by Miss Elizabeth Jordan in a short story called 'Varick's Lady o' Dreams.' Did the two later writers get the suggestion of it from Mr. Kipling or from Mr. Du Maurier? Did Mr. Kipling even get it from Mr. Du Maurier? Or did each of the four independently happen upon the tempting impossibility? It was Fitz James O'Brien who wrote 'What Was It?'—a thrilling tale of a strange creature, which could not be seen but could be felt; and Guy de Maupassant, in 'Le Horla,' introduces us to just such another uncanny and impossible monster, palpable but invisible. Did

the Frenchman borrow this weird impossibility from the Irish-American who had
invented it thirty years earlier? Or did he
reinvent it for himself? No wonder is it
that Mr. Austin Dobson asks:

> Ah, World of ours, are you so **gray**
> And weary, World, of spinning,
> That you repeat the tales to-day
> You told at the beginning?
> For lo! the same old myths that **made**
> The early stage-successes,
> Still hold the boards and still are **played**
> "With new effects and dresses."

Students of folk-lore seem to be agreed
—if indeed they are in accord about anything at all—that certain kinds of stories
are likely to spring up spontaneously whenever and wherever the conditions are favor-
able, while tales of a different type are
apparently transmitted swiftly and myste-
riously from one country and one language
to another land and another tongue. It
was Whewell who asserted that all the Irish
bulls had been calves in Greece; and it was
Professor Tyrrel who neatly explained that

the Irish bull differed from the bull of all other islands in that "it was always pregnant."

To trace these similarities, accidental as they are mostly, or intentional as they may be sometimes, is gratifying to the detective instinct, and it is an amusement harmless enough if we do not exaggerate the importance of our chance finds, and if we recognize fully the right of every man to profit by all that has been accomplished by his predecessors. Every generation has the privilege of standing on the shoulders of the generation that went before; but it has no right to pick the pockets of the first-comer. In an earlier paper on the 'Ethics of Plagiarism' the present writer suggested that the man who finds a new idea deserves the full credit of fresh invention; that the second user of this idea may possibly be considered a plagiarist; that the third person to utilize it is only lacking in originality, and that the fourth is merely drawing from the common stock. "And when the fifth man takes it, that's research!" was the apt comment of a philosophic friend.

The preceding paragraphs may perhaps appear to provide a portico somewhat too pretentious for the modest inquiry which is to follow. Their purpose was but to make it clear that this modest inquiry was not undertaken with any intent to denounce the crime of plagiarism. Its object is rather to show how many forms a pleasant conceit may assume as it travels down the centuries and as it migrates from one language to another.

Some diligent readers of modern verse may chance to be acquainted with a triolet of the late W. E. Henley's, which turns upon the ease with which a triolet can be written:

> Easy is the triolet,
>   If you really learn to make it!
> Once a neat refrain you get,
> Easy is the triolet.
> As you see!—I pay my debt
>   With another rhyme. Deuce take it,
> Easy is the triolet,
>   If you really learn to make it!

21

Probably more than one of those who may have glanced at this pleasantly phrased trifle recalled a rondeau of Mr. Austin Dobson's, which also found its subject-matter in the conditions of the form itself:

> You bid me try, Blue-Eyes, to write
> A Rondeau. What!—forthwith?—To-night?
> Reflect. Some skill I have, 'tis true;—
> But thirteen lines!—and rhymed on two!
> "I must," you say. Ah, hapless plight!
> Still, there are five lines,—ranged aright.
> These Gallic bonds, I feared, would fright
> My easy muse. They did till you—
>> *You* bid me try!
> That makes them niné. The port's in sight;—
> 'Tis all because your eyes are bright!
> Now just a pair to end with "oo,"—
> When maids command, what can't we do!
> Behold!—the Rondeau, tasteful, light,
>> You bid me try!

But Mr. Dobson, as is his wont, was scrupulously careful to put forth his rondeau in English as a free imitation of a rondeau in French by Voiture:

> Ma foy; c'est fait de moy. Car Isabeau
> M'a conjuré de luy faire un Rondeau.
>> Cela me met en une peine extrême.
>> Quoy, treize vers, huit en eau, cinq en ême!

Je luy ferois aussi tot un bateau.
En violà cinq, pourtant, en un monceau;
Faisons-en huict, en invoquant Brodeau,
Et puis mettons, par quelque stratagème,
    Ma foy, c'est fait.
Si je pouvois encore de mon cerveau
Tirer cinq vers, l'ouvrage seroit beau.
    Mais cependant, je suis dedans l'onzième,
    Et si je croy que je fais le douzième,
En voilà treize ajustés au niveau.
    Ma foy, c'est fait!

And this raises the question whether in Voiture we have found the first versifier who filled a fixed form by an airy discussion of the difficulties to be overcome by all who adventure upon that form; and here the answer is easy. Voiture was apparently only the first lyrist to rhyme a rondeau of this sort; for he had as a predecessor Desmarets, who had used this device to help him in the composition of a sonnet. And it is asserted that the Frenchman had borrowed the conceit from an Italian, Marini, a most voluminous sonneteer. Unfortunately, the present writer has not been able to lay hands on Marini's sonnet, or on

23

that of Desmarets, despite a diligent search. But the finding of the French lyric, and of the Italian that suggested it, is of less importance, since there is no doubt that both of them were derived from a Spanish original.

In his 'New Art of Making Plays' Lope de Vega advised the dramaturgic novice that the sonnet-form was well-fitted for soliloquies; but, although this particular sonnet is to be found in one of his plays, 'La Nina de Plata,' it is not a soliloquy, being recited by the *gracioso* or comedian, frankly as a poetic composition.

SONETO A VIOLANTE.

Un soneto me manda hacer Violante:
   Que en me vida me he visto en tanto aprieto;
   Catorce versos dicen que es soneto:
Burla burlando van los tres delante;
Yo pensé que no hallára consonante,
   Y estoy a la mitad de otro cuarteto;
   Mas si me veo en el primer terceto;
No hay cosa en los cuartetos que me espante
En el primer terceto voy entrando,
   Y aun parece que entré con pié derecho,

A THEME, WITH VARIATIONS

Pues fin con este verso le voy dando;
Ya estoy en el segundo, y aun sospecho
Que voy los trece versos acabando;
Contad si son catorce: ya está hecho.

In his study of the life and works of the great Spanish playwright, Lord Holland quoted an English adaptation of Lope's Spanish original, written by a certain Thomas Edwards, the author of a carefully forgotten discussion of the 'Canons of Criticism,' these canons being weapons of offence primed and aimed to blow Warburton off the face of the earth. This lawyer-critic refused to bind himself down to the strict Guittonian form of the sonnet; and his wit was not over nimble; but he managed to get his fourteen rhymes in presentable shape:

Capricious Wray a sonnet needs must have:
    I ne'er was so put to't before—a sonnet?
    Why, fourteen verses must be spent upon it.
'Tis good, however, I've conquer'd the first stave.
    Yet I shall ne'er find rhvmes enough by half,
Said I, and found myself in the midst of the second:
If twice four verses were fairly reckon'd
    I should turn back on the hardest part, and laugh.

Thus far with good success I think I've scribbled,
And of twice seven lines have clear got o'er ten.
  Courage! Another'll finish the first triplet;
Thanks to the muse, my work begins to shorten,
  There's thirteen lines got through, driblet by drib-
    let,
'Tis done! count how you will, I warrant there's
  fourteen.

There is a conscientious rigidity about
this sturdy British sonneteer and an
eighteenth-century stiffness about his sacri-
fice to the muse which contrast sharply with
the Gallic vivacity and the nineteenth-cen-
tury expertness to be found in a sonnet by
the late Henri Meilhac (the collaborator of
M. Ludovic Halévy, in the composition of
the 'Belle Hélène,' of the 'Grande Duch-
esse de Gerolstein' and of the 'Perichole').
No one can now declare with certainty
whether Meilhac borrowed the suggestion
from Desmarets or Voiture, his predecessors in his own tongue, or whether he took
it over from the Italian or from the
Spanish. In fact, Meilhac was quite ingenious enough to have invented the device for

his own use; and his sonnet has the brilliancy and the buoyancy which we expect to find in the best *vers de société:*

UN SONNET.

Un Sonnet, dites-vous; savez-vous bien, Madame,
  Qu'il me faudra trouver trois rimes à sonnet?
Madame, heureusement, rime avec âme et flamme,
  Et le premier quatrain me semble assez complet.

J'entame le second, le second je l'ent‥me,
  Et prends en l'entament un air tout guilleret,
Car ne m'étant encor point servi du mot âme,
  Je compte m'en servir, et m'en sers, en effet.

Vous m'accorderez bien, maintenant, j'imagine,
Qu'un sonnet sans amour ferait fort triste mine,
  Qu'il aurait l'air boiteux, contrefait, mal tourné.

Il nous faut de l'amour, il nous en faut quand même;
J'écris donc en tremblant; je vous aime, ou je t'aime,
  Et voilà, pour le coup, mon sonnet terminé.

It was Meilhac's sonnet which the late Henry Cuyler Bunner paraphrased, carrying over into English, so far as might be possible, not only the fundamental conceit but also the most of the minor felicities of the French lyrist. Bunner's 'Sonnet to Order' was avowedly an imitation; and, when it was first published in an American magazine, it was accompanied by its French original:

A sonnet would you have? Know you, my pet,
   For sonnets fourteen lines are necessary.
   Ah, *necessary* rhymes, by luck, to *fairy*—
I'll call you one, and the first quatrain get.
This meets half-way the second; half-way met,
   One meets an obstacle in a manner airy.
   But here, though it is not your name, as Mary
I'll set you down, settling the second set.

Now, you'll admit, a sonnet without love,
   Without the savor of a woman in't,
     Were profanation of poetic art.
Love, above all things! So 'tis writ above.
   Nor there alone. Your sonneteer, I'd hint,
     Gives you this sonnet here with all his heart.

One of the scholarly contributors to Petit de Julleville's history of the French language and literature remarked that "nothing is longer than a sonnet—when there is nothing in it"; and here we have had some half-dozen sonnets with only one thought

in the lot of them. Yet another is called
'A Difficult Sonnet'; and it was found amid
the flotsam and jetsam of a scrap-book,
credited vaguely to the *University Magazine*, and seemingly clipped out some twenty or thirty years ago. It does not quite
continue the tradition that has here been
traced down through the modern languages;
indeed, the obvious desire of the poet to
moralize points to an English lyrist who
believed in his own originality:

With an idea I set to write a sonnet;
  The subject was so difficult and terse,
  I could not quite bring right the tiresome verse,
Much labor though I spent, and pens, upon it:
Still I plod on, and line by line I con it,
  Each time with better words to add, or worse,
  Till it comes right; and, as I last rehearse
The settled stanza, make fair copy on it. .
This done, I take my blotted rough endeavor,
  Covering some sheets with every kind of scrawl
Of my first failures, some of them quite clever;
  Into a little pack I bring them all,
Tear up. (Life is the Poem—where's the taper?
How shall I burn my blotted bits of paper?

The triolet, the rondeau, and the sonnet
have each in turn been taken by lyrists who

wished thus to exploit their own playfulness; and the ballade is the only other fixed form of verse likely to prove equally tempting. But a conscientious search has failed to find any ballade turning on the difficulty of making a ballade, with its three octaves, its envoy, its refrain, and its three rhymes, repeated and interlaced. In 'Cyrano de Bergerac,' M. Rostand makes his hero improvise a ballade while he is fighting a duel —a gorgeous example of bravado and bravura; and the verses, purporting to be put together in the very moment of deadly combat, abound in allusions to the structure of the ballade itself. And yet the basis of M. Rostand's ballade, with its refrain "*à la fin de l'envoi, je touche,*" does not differ much from that of Lope de Vega, although the superstructure of the later lyric achieves a certain originality. There are at least two English translations of M. Rostand's play; but any rendering of the flashing lines of the flamboyant original cannot but seem a little pale. Who was it first asserted that a translated poem was like a boiled strawberry?

Of all the Teutonic tongues our own English is the almost only one which has taken part in these international borrowings. Students of German poetry, and of Dutch, have been unable to answer the appeal for kindred lyrics from these languages.

In Danish—so a kind correspondent in Copenhagen has informed me—there is a sonnet "by request" from the pen of Johan Ludvig Heiberg (1791-1860). He was a student of Spanish literature, and he presents his own poem as an imitation of a Spanish original:

SONET (efter Mendoza)

I ønsker en Sonet. Som I befaler!
Det første med det andet Vers er skrevet,
Og er ei Nummer Tre tilskamme blevet,
Med fjerde Vers jeg een Qvartet betaler.

Jeg kommer til det femte. Hjelp! Jeg daler!
Sanct Jacob! Marche! Det sjette fremad drevet!
Hvis jeg det syvende kun faaer oplevet,
Har jeg dog Livet frelst af disse Qvaler!

31

Nu er jeg færdig med de to Qvartetter.
Hvad synes jer! Forstaaer jeg mig at vende?
Men Himlen veed, jeg skjælver for Tercetter!

Og hvis jeg kan med Ære slutte denne,
Jeg skriver i mit Liv ei fleer Sonetter,
Da denne første, Gud skee Lov, fik Ende!

Until this Danish lyric came to light, it seemed as though the original inventor of the pleasant device was indisputably Lope de Vega (1562-1635). But Heiberg gives the credit to the author of the earliest picaresque romance 'Lazarillo de Tormes', Diego Hurtando de Mendoza, the brilliant historian (1503-1575), who died when Lope was but a boy of thirteen. And just after the Danish sonnet had reached me, another kind correspondent sent me from Idaho this English version of Mendoza's original, translated by Matthew Russell:—

THE SONNET.

You ask a sonnet, lady, and behold!
The first line and the second are complete.
If equal luck I in the third should meet,
With one verse more the first quatrain is told.

A THEME, WITH VARIATIONS

St. James for Spain! the fifth verse is outrolled—
Now for the sixth. 'Twill be a gallant feat
If after all I manage to retreat
Safe with my life from this encounter bold.

Already, rounded well, each quatrain stands.
What say you, lady? Do I bravely speed?
Yet, ah! heaven knows the tercets me affright;

And if this sonnet were but off my hands,
Another I should ne'er attempt, indeed.
But now, thank God, my sonnet's finished quite.

Apparently the Northern tongues have not taken so kindly to the fixed forms as the Southern languages did. And yet no example of a lyric containing this conceit has been forthcoming from Portuguese or from Provençal. This last deficiency is the more remarkable, since the origin of all the fixed forms has been traced to that home of minstrelsy. The sonnet was invented by a Provençal lyrist, just as the rondeau was, and the ballade also.

The sonnet established itself first, and gained the widest acceptance; and it is only of late that the rondeau and the ballade have achieved a certain popularity, far

33

inferior to that of the sonnet. Indeed, of all the fixed forms the sonnet is at once the best known and the most noble. It has been used to convey the loftiest of messages; it has done this successfully without calling undue attention to the necessary artifice of its construction. The rondeau, on the other hand, and the ballade also, have seemed best fitted for lighter themes of minor importance. They carry more appropriately the ingenious prettiness of *vers de société;* whereas the sonnet has proved itself to be worthy of the most elevated thcmes.

. In seeking to discover what poet it was who first devised a lyric in a fixed form, turning on the arbitrary difficulty of the form itself, there is no need to go further back than the Renascence, since the fixed form was a product of the Renascence, impossible until after rhyme had been elaborated in the Middle Ages. In the lyrics of Rome and Greece, with all their exquisite modulations of metre, there was

34

no rhyme; and therefore no fixed form was possible, built upon an artful adjustment of repeated and contrasted rhymes.

In Hebrew versification, it ought to be noted here, the acrostic was held in high esteem. Perchance there exists in Hebrew an acrostic, setting forth the difficulty to be vanquished by every bard who seeks to write an acrostic.

(1903.)

P. S.—There is a motto popular in the minor marts of trade: "If you don't see what you want, ask for it." And the original publication of this inquiry promptly moved an anonymous British bard to provide the needed ballade based on the difficulty of its own structure. He called it a 'Ballade in the Making.'

> Do you desire me, friend, to write
>   The Ballade of Clément Marot,
> And incidentally indite
>   The lines on which it ought to go?
>   Then, firstly, I would have you know,
> One must be gifted with resource,
>   For, like the Rondel and Rondeau,
> The Ballade is a *tour de force*.

35

RECREATIONS OF AN ANTHOLOGIST

Three rhymes you need; but choose aright,
    For one (like this of mine in "O")
Comes fourteen times; then find a bright
    Refrain, and keep it *mot pour mot*
    To fall spontaneously below
Each of three septets; this, of course,
    Needs ingenuity, for oh!
The Ballade is a *tour de force.*

Think not to find the task as light
    As Rostand tells did Cyrano,
Composing octaves through a fight
    And envoy as he pinked his foe.
    Remember, too, your verse should flow
Smooth as a river from its source—
    So smooth, in fact, as not to show
⌐he Ballade is a *tour de force.*

L'ENVOI.
Envoy, addressed to so-and-so,
    Should all that goes before indorse,
As thus:—O reader mine, I trow
    The Ballade is a *tour de force.*

III

UNWRITTEN BOOKS

TO most of the admirers of Dickens the 'Mystery of Edwin Drood' remains still a mystery, since the author died suddenly and before he had himself disclosed his own answer to his serial conundrum. We may give as many guesses as we choose, we cannot be absolutely certain that our solution of the problem is the real one. Thackeray was far above any mystery-mongering of this sort, and he scorned to entrap his readers into puzzling over a mere enigma of plot; but he had acquired from Dickens the inartistic habit of beginning the intermittent publication of a novel before he had composed the final chapters, and 'Denis Duval' remains to us an interrupted beginning of what might have been a

worthy companion of 'Henry Esmond.'
More than one attempt was made to complete Dickens's broken narrative, but no
rash writer was hardy enough to venture
on a continuation of Thackeray's novel.
When Wilkie Collins left a serial unfinished, Sir Walter Besant kindly supplied
a conclusion; and Mr. Quiller-Couch did
a like friendly service for Robert Louis
Stevenson.

Here in America Hawthorne tried three
times to get his strange story of the bloody
footstep into a shape satisfactory to his
fastidious sense of form, and he allowed
'The Dolliver Romance' to begin to appear
in a magazine before he had completed
the manuscript. The sudden death of
Dickens and of Thackeray was his also,
and his instalment of life in this world
was sharply cut off—to be continued in
our next. As in Thackeray's case, so in
Hawthorne's, the impossibility of com-
pleting what the master had begun was so
plain that even the most foolishly con-

ceited have restrained their pens from the task. As Hawthorne's classmate, Longfellow, beautifully phrased it:

> There, in seclusion and remote from men,
> The wizard hand lies cold,
> Which at its topmost speed let fall the pen,
> And left the tale half-told.
>
> Ah! who shall lift that wand of magic power,
> And the lost clue regain?
> The unfinished window in Aladdin's tower
> Unfinished must remain.

Hawthorne, however, and Thackeray had at least begun these books; the 'Dolliver Romance' and 'Denis Duval' remain unfinished, but they were not absolutely unwritten. There are in the records of literature other books by other authors actually announced as these were, but never even begun. Some of these unwritten books may have been thought out, composed, ready to be set down in black and white with pen and ink, complete in the author's head, and lacking the final and almost mechanical registration. Others seem to have been mere projects, little more than vague dreams, for a possible future realisation. At one stage of its existence every book is but a castle in the air; and, the persevering author acts on Thoreau's assertion, that the air is the proper place for a castle, and that what needs to be done is only to build a solid foundation under it.

Molière is said by most of his biographers to have made a translation from Lucretius; and if this ever really existed it is now lost. But another of Molière's works never did exist—the comedy of 'L'Homme de Cour'—which he used to talk about as certain to be his final masterpiece, but of which nothing is now known. So Richard Brinsley Sheridan made ready to write a successor to the 'Rivals' and the 'School for Scandal,' on the theme of 'Affectation,' but this admirable subject did not tempt him to the actual labor of composition. He made a few notes for the proposed play, and pursued it no further. Perhaps he was too absorbed in the pleasures of society or in the delights of politics; perhaps he was satisfied with the comedies he had already written and willing to rest his title to remembrance upon these. Michael Kelly tells us how he once said to Sheridan that the manager of Drury Lane would never write another comedy, since he was afraid—afraid of the author of the 'School for Scandal,' And like Molière and like Sheridan, Cervantes had projected a final play, destined to eclipse all its predecessors—'Engaño a los Ojos'—and yet not destined to see the light of day, since the author of 'Don Quixote' died before it was ready, if indeed it was ever begun.

For years the paper covers of every new book that Victor Hugo issued continued to announce as soon to be published a romance entitled 'La Quinquengrogne.' Many posthumous volumes of the French poet's writing in prose and verse have been sent forth by his literary executors, but of this oddly entitled fiction nothing has been heard. Théophile Gautier's 'Capitaine Fracasse' was proclaimed as almost ready for print for many long years before the first word of it was actually written; but at last Gautier did write up to his title. Which one of his Romanticist companions in arms was it who achieved instant fame on his declaration of intention to astound the world sooner or later with a treatise, 'Sur l'Incommodité des Commodes?'—a treatise which, like a bill in Congress, has been read by title only.

In 1862, Alphonse Daudet in like manner announced as "in press" a volume of stories, which was to be called 'Le Pentaméron,' and which remained unpublished and probably unwritten when he died in 1897. A novel of Daudet's—'Trousseaux et Layettes'—about which he was in the habit of conversing with his intimates in the later years of his life, seems to have been begun, but apparently it was not very far advanced when death overtook him. And the younger Dumas has left on record more than one reference to a comedy to be called 'La Route de Thèbes', planned before 'Francillon,' but never brought to the point of perfection during the author's lifetime.

In the original prospectus of M. Jules Jusserand's admirable series of critical biographies, 'Les Grands Ecrivains Français,' it was asserted that M. Anatole France would contribute the volume on Racine and M. Jules Lemaître that on Alfred de Musset. But when the time came to publish the book on Racine its author was found to be not M. France, but M. Gustave Larroumet; and the volume on Musset was prepared, not by M. Lemaître, but by Mme. Arvède Barine. Boileau was to have been undertaken by M. Ferdinand Brunetière, and Rousseau by the late Victor Cherbuliez; but M. Gustave Lanson was the author of the account of the great classic critic, and M.

Chuquet was responsible for the biography of the progenitor of French Romanticism. It is more than ten years since the prospectus of this series was prepared, and M. Brunetière has not yet given us his promised study of Voltaire, nor has M. Paul Bourget vouchsafed us his analysis of Balzac.

Taine was to have written the life of Sainte-Beuve for this series, but he died before he had accomplished the pleasant and appropriate task. In like manner Lowell at the time of his death had made little progress with the volume on Hawthorne which he had agreed to prepare for the corresponding series in this country, Mr. Warner's 'American Men of Letters'; and to an American in London, with whom he was talking over his theme, Lowell expressed his gentle dissatisfaction with the volume on Hawthorne contributed to the 'English Men of Letters' by Mr. Henry James. Lowell remarked that Hawthorne was of New England, all

44

compact, and could be treated adequately only by a New Englander, whereas Mr. James, in so far as he was an American at all, was a New Yorker.

The 'American Men of Letters' series has had almost as many substitutions as the 'Grands Ecrivains Français.' Mr. Thomas Bailey Aldrich was to have written the volume on N. P. Willis, and Professor Beers did write it. Mr. George W. Cable undertook to prepare an account of William Gilmore Simms, and Professor Trent did prepare it. Mr. Howells was expected to write the life of Longfellow, and Colonel Higginson took it over. And in the original prospectus of the corresponding British series, the earliest of the three, Mr. John Morley's 'English Men of Letters,' the editor reserved to himself two authors, Gray and Burke. The study of Burke he has published, but that of Gray he turned over to Mr. Gosse. And the volume on Berkeley which the late Professor Huxley was to prepare for Mr. Mor-

ley's series never got itself written, although
that on Hume did.

It was more or less in rivalry with Mr.
Morley's series that Mr. Andrew Lang
began a collection of 'English Worthies,'
which the editor himself was to provide
with a biography of Izaak Walton—a
project abandoned apparently when the
series itself was given up. And it was
for this set of 'English Worthies' that
Robert Louis Stevenson made ready to
celebrate the deeds of Wellington, as un-
likely a subject as could well be chosen
by him—although his master, Scott, had
made money by a huge book about Na-
poleon. When one of Stevenson's intimates—one of his collaborators, indeed
—was asked why the victor of Waterloo
had been selected by the author of the
'Strange Case of Dr. Jekyll and Mr. Hyde,'
the laughing answer was, "Oh, Louis
thinks he has an eye for strategy and
tactics."

To the excellent series of 'History and

Literature Primers,' which was edited by
J. R. Green, the historian, and which contains the extraordinarily successful primer
of English literature by Mr. Stopford
Brooke and the equally illuminative primer
of Greek literature by Professor Jebb,
Dean Farrar was to contribute a primer
of Latin literature. And to a kindred
series of little books on 'Classical Writers,'
Professor James Bryce had promised a
study of Herodotus. Both of these books,
now overdue for more than half a score
of years, remain unwritten.

And what has become of the 'Book of
the Forty-five Mornings'—most alluring
title—which Mr. Rudyard Kipling dangled
before our eyes almost as long ago?
Everything comes to him who waits, but
have we not waited long enough for this?

Perhaps one or another of these unwritten books by men of letters still alive
may get themselves into print all in good
time; and, perhaps, none of them will ever
see the light. And it may be that their

authors are wise in their own generation, in so far as they may prefer the contemplation of a possibility never to be attempted to any effort to possess a reality that might be a bitter disappointment. No unwritten book can ever be a reproach to an author or a burden to his friends, nor can it gratify his enemies. No unwritten poem can be picked to pieces by criticasters. No unwritten play can be damned by faint praise. As Scribe, that wiliest of playwrights, once declared, "What is cut out is never hissed." What is unwritten cannot be abused offensively, nor can it be eulogized effusively—which to a sincere author may be even more distasteful.

No author was ever more frankly sincere than Whittier; and it was Whittier who wrote:

> Let the thick curtain fall;
> I better know than all
> How little I have gained,
> How vast the unattained.

UNWRITTEN BOOKS

Sweeter than any sung
My songs that found no tongue,
Nobler than any fact
My wish that failed the act.

Others shall sing the song,
Others shall right the wrong—
Finish what I begin—
And all I fail of, win.

(1899).

IV

SEED-CORN FOR STORIES

IN the characteristic little book of
little essays which Mr. Aldrich has
chosen to call 'Ponkapog Papers'
there are half a hundred pages of
'Asides'—fragmentary and unrelated paragraphs, compounded of cleverness and
shrewdness and wit. In reading these
pages we feel almost as though the author
had permitted us to peep into his note-
book; and we find ourselves wondering
whether our manners ought not to bid us
close the volume. These 'Asides' seem
to be far less labored and less self-conscious
than the 'Marginalia,' most of which Poe
chipped out of the longer essays and reviews that he did not care to reprint in
full.

Mr. Aldrich tells us that in the blotted

memorandum-book from which he has chosen these chance paragraphs, there are a score or two of suggestions for essays and for sketches and for poems which he has not written and which he never will write. "The instant I jot down an idea," he informs us, "the desire to utilize it leaves me, and I turn away to do something unpremeditated. The shabby volume has become a sort of Potter's Field where I bury my intentions, good and bad, without any belief in their final resurrection." As if in proof of this confession, Mr. Aldrich has included among these 'Asides' two or three suggestions, which he does not intend to utilize himself and which he generously presents to the public. They are seed-corn for stories which he has not cared to plant and tend and harvest himself.

Here is one of these undeveloped imaginings:

"In his memoirs, Krapotkin states the singular fact that the natives of the Malayan Archipelago have an idea that something is extracted from them when their likenesses are taken by photography. Here is the motive for a fantastic short-story, in which the hero—an author in vogue or a popular actor—might be depicted as having all his good qualities gradually photographed out of him. This could well be the result of a too prolonged indulgence in the effort to 'look natural.' First the man loses his charming simplicity; then he begins to pose in intellectual attitudes, with finger on brow; then he becomes morbidly self-conscious, and finally ends in an asylum for incurable egotists."

And here is a second as appallingly imaginative as the first was humorously fanciful: "Imagine all human beings swept off the face of the earth, excepting one man. Imagine this man in some vast city, New York or London. Imagine him on the third or fourth day of his solitude sitting in a house and hearing a ring at the door-bell!"

As we read this we cannot but wonder

whether the bare idea thus boldly thrown
out is not more powerful than any more
amply wrought tale could be, even if it
was to be told with all Mr. Aldrich's own
delicate ingenuity. And then we wonder
whether the author refrained from writing
this story himself for the reason he has
given us,—that he tired of his own suggestions so soon as he got them down in
black and white—or whether in this case
his generosity to the public is not due to
the intuitive feeling of an accomplished
craftsman that the naked notion, stark and
unadorned, is more striking and more powerful in its simplicity than it would be if
it was elaborated according to all the pre-
cepts of the art of fiction.

In Poe's 'Marginalia' there is one passage in some measure akin to Mr. Aldrich's
second suggestion. "I have sometimes
amused myself," the poet declared, "by
endeavoring to fancy what would be the
fate of an individual gifted, or rather
accursed, with an intellect *very* far supe-

rior to that of his race. Of course he would be conscious of his superiority; nor could he (if otherwise constituted as man is) help manifesting his consciousness. Thus he would make enemies at all points. And—since his opinions and speculations would widely differ from those of all mankind—that he would be considered as a madman, is evident. How horribly painful such a condition! Hell could invent no greater torture than that of being charged with abnormal weakness on account of being abnormally strong."

Here again the suggestion itself in its bare simplicity is more effective than any completed story. But there is another of Poe's notions which seems not so difficult of treatment and which he might very readily have carried out. He called it 'A Suggestion for a Magazine Article.'

"Here is a good idea for a magazine paper; let somebody 'work it up.' A flippant pretender to universal acquirement —a would-be Crichton—engrosses, for an hour or two, perhaps, the attention of a large company, most of whom are profoundly impressed by his knowledge. He is very witty, in especial, at the expense of a modest young gentleman, who ventures to make no reply, and who, finally, leaves the room as if overwhelmed with confusion; the Crichton greeting his exit with a laugh. Presently he returns, followed by a footman carrying an armful of books. These are deposited on the table. The young gentleman now, referring to some pencilled notes which he had been secretly taking during the Crichton's display of erudition, pins the latter to his statements, each by each, and refutes them all in turn, by reference to the very authorities cited by the egotist himself, whose ignorance at all points is thus made apparent."

With characteristic affectation Poe insisted that his 'Marginalia' had been written in his books, on the margins themselves when these happened to be ample enough, and on a slip of paper deposited between the leaves when what he had to note was "too much to be included within the narrow limits of a margin." He admitted this to be a whim, and declared that it might "be not only a very hackneyed, but a very idle practice," but he asserted that he persisted in it because it afforded him pleasure. He maintained that "the purely marginal jottings, done with no eye to the Memorandum Book, have a distinct complexion, and not only not a distinct purpose, but none at all; this it is which imparts to them a value." Unfortunately for Poe's claim that in these fragmentary notes he was talking "freshly, boldly, originally," his editors have been able to trace the most of his paragraphs to articles of his which he did not care to reprint in full. As Mr. Stedman explains, "they afforded the magazinist an easy way of making copy," since "they were largely made up of passages lifted from earlier essays and reviews." And Mr. Stedman also points out how

Poe's pretence that his 'Marginalia' are what their prelude and title imply, "is made transparent by their formal, premeditated style, so different from that of Hawthorne's 'Note-Books,' or that of Thoreau's posthumous apothegms and reflections."

It is the charm of Hawthorne's 'Note-Books' that they really were written for himself alone and with no thought of publication. Although he went to them for material for the book about his English sojourn, 'Our Old Home,' and although he picked out of them many an idea which he worked up in a tale or in a romance, he kept them for his own eye only. As his widow asserted when she made a selection from these journals for publication several years after his death, he was "entertaining, and not asserting, opinions and ideas." She insisted that her husband was questioning, doubting and reflecting with his pen, and, as it were, instructing himself,—so that his note-books should be read "not as definitive conclusions of his mind, but merely as passing impressions often."

The later journals kept in Great Britain, in France and in Italy are entertaining because they give us the impressions of Hawthorne himself, recorded at the moment of reception often; but they are far less interesting and less valuable than the note-books he filled in his youth before he had ever left his native land. Here we get very close to him; we see his mind at work; we trace the first hint of a story as he jots it down and we can see it growing as it takes root in his mind. For example, the idea of the 'Virtuoso's Collection' came to him again and again in slightly different forms; and as we turn the pages of his note-books we can discover when it was that he happened upon one and another of the marvellous curiosities which enriched the strange gathering. In like manner the first suggestion of that characteristic tale, the 'Birthmark,' is set down in three lines, which tell the whole story: "A person to be in possession of something as perfect as mortal man has a right to demand; he tries to make it better, and ruins it entirely."

Sometimes the suggestion is merely fanciful, and too diaphanous to withstand elaboration: "A person to catch fire-flies, and try to kindle his household fire with them. It would be symbolical of something." Sometimes the suggestion is bold enough and alluring, but not to be accomplished without a complicated machinery, which would detract from its directness: "The situation of a man in the midst of a crowd, yet as completely in the power of another, life and all, as they two were in the deepest solitude." Sometimes the suggestion is so characteristic, so individual, so Hawthornesque, that we find ourselves wondering how it was that it did not tempt Hawthorne himself to its ampler unfolding: "A person to be writing a tale, and to find that it shapes itself

59

against his intentions; that the characters
act otherwise than he thought; that unfore-
seen events occur; and a catastrophe comes
which he strives in vain to avert. It might
shadow forth his own fate—he having
made himself one of the personages." Or
this: "Follow out the fantasy of a man
taking his life by instalments, instead of
at one payment,—say ten years of life
alternately with ten years of suspended
animation." Of course this last idea has
a certain kinship with 'Rip van Winkle'
and with the 'Man with the Broken Ear;'
but it differs in that Hawthorne supposes
his hero to act voluntarily and more than
once, whereas there was but a single and
involuntary suspension of animation in
Irving's tale and in About's.

Another of Hawthorne's suggestions he
might have treated himself, no doubt, with
the delicate aroma of pure romance; but
the theme would also lend itself to a wholly
different treatment, by a novelist enamored
of real things and of the externals of life:

"A story, the hero of which is to be represented as naturally capable of deep and strong passion, and looking forward to the time when he shall feel passionate love, which is to be the great event of his existence. But it so chances that he never falls in love, and although he gives up the expectation of so doing, and marries calmly, yet it is somewhat sadly, with sentiments merely of esteem for his bride. The lady might be one who had loved him early in life, but whom then, in his expectation of passionate love, he had scorned."

No doubt more than one of these suggestions fructified in the minds of one or another reader of Hawthorne's 'Note-Books' who happened also to be writers of fiction. If the present writer may offer himself as a witness, or if he may be allowed to enter the confessional, he admits that a short-story of his composition, 'Esther Feverel,' was only an attempt to carry out a hint of Hawthorne's: "An old looking-glass; somebody finds out the secret of making all the images that have been reflected in it pass back again across its surface." And everybody knows that it was a story told to Hawthorne by a friend, and duly entered in the 'Note-Books' which he abandoned to his classmate Longfellow to treat in verse as 'Evangeline.'

In the volume of essays and sketches of travel which Mr. Howells has called 'Literature and Life,' and to which he gave an accurate sub-title when he characterized them as 'Studies,' there is one article containing the plot for a story. The paper is named 'Worries of a Winter Walk' and it narrates how Mr. Howells, in his pilgrimages about New York, went over toward the East River and came "upon a bit of our motley life, a fact of our piebald civilization," which perplexed him and which suggested a little love-story. He tells us how the first notion of the tale occurred to him, evoked by an unexpected fact he had observed; and then with lam-

bent humor he traces the succcessive steps
by which the story grew in his mind, as
it slowly took shape and began to have
an independent existence. It was an idyl
of the East Side, a kodak-picture snapped
in the midst of our cosmopolitan conglom-
eration of foreign peoples here in this
crowded island. Mr. Howells sets forth
one after another the variations of the
little tale in his own mind, those which he
decided to reject as well as those which he
accepted. And finally he presents us with
three possible terminations of the story, as
though in doubt himself which was in fact
the best. The narrative is shot through
with the gentle irony and with the honest
self-detachment so characteristic of the
creator of 'Silas Lapham.'

In the end we find that he has not actually written out his story; he has merely
told us how he might have written it. But
the tale is complete; and we can see for
ourselves—if only we bring our share of
sympathetic imagination—how it would

read if he had chosen to tell it simply as
he has told his other stories. To the
reader to whom a story is only a story—
to the reader who is entertained only by
what has happened and who is interested
only in discovering how it turns out at last
—perhaps the irony and the self-detachment are a little disconcerting. But to the
scantier band who are alive to the subtle
relations of literature and life, the tale
thus presented is far more attractive than
if it had been presented in the author's
usual fashion. And this the author himself knew, with that understanding of the
difficulties of his craft which is part of his
equipment as a man of letters. The story
itself remains unwritten, but not unwrit-
able; and any other teller of tales who is
in search of a ready-made plot can have
it for the taking. But if any teller of
tales does borrow it from Mr. Howells's
book, and if he sets it forth in full as
though it had happened, he may rest as-
sured that his elaborative art is likely to

fail of achieving the successful result attained by Mr. Howells's skilful and tactful commingling of ingenious suggestion and playful irony.

If the present writer may again call himself as a witness, it will be to confess that in a certain little tale of his own, 'Love at First Sight,' containing only the conversation at dinner of a pretty girl with a young author, he scattered broadcast three several suggestions for stories,—and that his reason for this reckless liberality was solely because these suggestions seemed to him more effective as mere suggestions than they would have been had he done his best to work them out conscientiously. One was only an alluring title, to which, however, he had never been able to fit an appropriate plot: 'The Parrot that talked in his Sleep.' The second was the bare hint for a Hawthornesque sketch to be called 'At the End of his Tether,' and to describe how a collector of morbid taste brought together bits of the ropes with which notorious criminals had been hanged, only at the last to splice these together that he might hang himself. And the third, the 'Queen of the Living Chessmen,' was more fully developed, and the young writer of fiction was able to outline it to the pretty girl at dinner and to profit by her acute criticism. This third tale thus sketched out seemed to have dramatic possibilities of its own—possibilities which so strongly impressed the editor of the magazine to which the manuscript was first submitted, that he rejected 'Love at First Sight' with the remark that he would be glad to accept the 'Queen of the Living Chessmen' if the author would write that out as a story by itself.

Yet this is just what the author was too wary to attempt. He is quite willing that it should be undertaken by another pen; but he had his own reasons for believing that the notion had made its full effect when it was presented merely as a notion. And it is his belief that the apparent generosity of Mr. Howells and of Mr. Aldrich—and that of Poe also—when they gave away the themes for tales that they had invented and that they might have written themselves had they so chosen, was the result of a delicate perception of the fact that the bare theme itself is often as valuable as the fully clothed tale would be. The underlying principle which has governed them is well stated by the younger Dumas in his account of the circumstances which led him to rewrite a play brought to him by Emile de Girardin, the 'Supplice d'une Femme.'

Dumas declares that all he found in Girardin's play was a single and striking situation. "But a situation is not an idea," he explains. "An idea has a beginning, a middle and an end—an exposition, a development, and a conclusion. Anybody can happen on a dramatic situation; but this must be prepared for, made acceptable, made possible, and above all, untied logically." And then Dumas generously throws out the suggestion of a new and striking dramatic situation. "A young man asks the hand of a young woman. It is accorded to him. He marries her civilly and religiously; and at the very moment when he is about to take her away with him, he learns categorically that he has married his sister. That is a situation, isn't it? and most interesting! But find a way out of it! I give you a thousand guesses,—and I give you the situation if you want it. He who shall make a good play with this as his starting-point will be the veritable author of the piece, and I shall not urge my claim."

It is proof of Dumas's perfect understanding of all the conditions of the dramaturgic art, that when two young French authors took him at his word and actually made a play out of this suggestion of his, the piece, although acted by the admirable company of the Odéon, was promptly dismissed as impossible.

(1904).

V

AMERICAN SATIRES IN VERSE

LTHOUGH most of the historians of American literature have acknowledged that humor is abundant in the writings of our authors, and that this humor is distinctive and characteristic, having a quality of its own, easy enough to perceive, even if difficult to define, no one of these historians has as yet cared to consider at length the American contribution to that special form of humor which we call the satire in verse.

Of this form the earliest masters were Horace and Juvenal, although it is still a matter of dispute which of the two was the more successful in this field. Dryden, who appreciated both of them, and who had found his profit in a shrewd analysis of their methods, held for the later Latin poet, declaring that "the sauce of Juvenal is more poignant to create in us an appetite of reading him." And then the robust British bard carried still further this culinary figure of speech, asserting that "the meat of Horace is more nourishing; but the cookery of Juvenal more exquisite: so that, granting Horace to be the more general philosopher, we cannot deny that Juvenal was the greater poet—I mean in satire."

It is in his learned and acute 'Discourse concerning the Origin and Progress of Satire' that Dryden records these opinions; and in this same essay, one of the richest and most masterful of his critical papers, he gives full mead of praise to the French critic whose influence upon the satirists coming after him was almost as dominating as that of the earlier Roman practitioners of the art. "If I would only cross the seas," Dryden asserted, "I might find in France a living Horace and a Juvenal, in the person of the admirable Boileau; whose numbers are excellent, whose thoughts are just, whose language is pure, whose satire is pointed, and whose sense is close." Then the Englishman proceeded to pay to the Frenchman a compliment, which might well be bestowed on himself, saying that what Boileau "borrowed from the Ancients, he repays with usury of his own, in coin as good, and almost as universally valuable."

The obvious difference between the French satirist and his Roman predecessors is that they dealt with society at large, Horace gently laughing at the foibles of the hour, and Juvenal nobly scourging the deeper vices of his darker period, whereas Boileau was interested rather more in literature than in life, caring less for the diseases of the body politic than for lapses from the laws of taste and breaches of the rules of art. Here he was followed by Pope, who was far less fortunate in his choice of authors to attack.

The judgment of posterity has confirmed most of the contemporary decisions of Boileau; and the reputations he killed have stayed dead. Not so with Pope, who was ill-advised enough to choose as the heroes of his 'Dunciad,' Theobald and Colley Cibber, writers vulnerable enough, no doubt, but neither of them dunces by any possible extension of the word. Theobald, in fact, was one of the most intelligent of the earlier Shaksperian commentators; and Cibber, however absurd a figure he might make as poet-laureate, was the author not only of one of the most amusing autobiographies in the language, but also of at least one comedy which has survived on the stage for nearly two centuries.

Just as one British compiler, Dodd, in his comprehensive collection of English epigrams, did not care to include any specimens of American wit, so another British editor of a recent anthology of 'English Satires,' Mr. Oliphant Smeaton, has failed to reproduce a single American example, although in his critical introduction he mentions more than one of our authors with casual compliment. It may be that Mr. Smeaton deliberately determined to ignore the American efforts in this department of literature; but it is far more likely that he was blandly ignorant of the value and of the variety of American satire in verse. In each of the three main divisions of this interesting department of literature, in the genial satire of society, of which Horace set the example, in the broader and bolder satire of contemporary politics, of which Juvenal has left the unapproachable model, and in the more personal and purely literary satire, of which Boileau and Pope have been accepted as masters,—in each of these three contiguous fields of literary endeavor, American authors have adventured themselves with varying success.

It is in the first of these three divisions, in the satire of society, glancing wittily at the men and the manners and the morals of the hour, that our American versifiers

have advanced least frequently. Yet even
in this form of satire the last half of the
nineteenth century saw the publication of
the late William Allen Butler's 'Nothing
to Wear,' of Mr. Stedman's brisk and
brilliant 'Diamond Wedding,' of Judge
Grant's ingenious 'Little Tin Gods on
Wheels,' and of the adroitly rhymed 'Bunt-
ling Ball,' generally ascribed to the late
Edgar Fawcett. In the first half of the century Halleck and Drake printed in a New
York evening paper the series of lively
lyrics which came to be known as the
'Croaker Papers'—the collaborating authors having chosen to sign their smart
rhymes with the name of a character in
Goldsmith's 'Good-natured Man.' Unfortunately for the fame of the associated
bards, their themes were very local and
of little lasting importance, so that it is
almost impossible to copy here any of their
clever verses without an apparatus of notes
explaining the allusions. What is very
contemporary is likely to be only tempo-

rary; and the up-to-date is soon seen to be out-of-date. A joke is no longer alluring when it demands a diagram in elucidation of its point.

A few years after the 'Croaker Papers' had astonished and delighted all New York, there was published at least one formal satire of society, prepared in full acceptance of all the precedents which govern a metrical attack on the follies and on the vices of the moment. This is 'Gotham and the Gothamites. A Medley. New York: 1823. Published for the Author.' For a New Yorker at the beginning of the twentieth century, loving this motley and mighty city of ours for what it is already and also for what it is to be in the future, there is not a little hardship in being forced to withhold high praise from a bard who set forth the pictorial charm of the town as it was four score years ago:

Beautiful city! like Venus from the deep,
All glowing in her beauty, dost thou spring

From out the waters, that murmuring creep
  Around thy island-throne, and proudly bring
Unto thy footstool, all that gorgeous stream
  Of pomp—of wealth—of richer merchandise;
The world's high homage! Yea, and I have seen
  The mighty sun o'er thy tall spires arise,
Pavillioned in his glory; and no sight
  Was lovelier. . . . .

After this unexpected pæan on the beauties of Manhattan, which are even now only grudgingly admitted, there is cause for sorrow in the later passages of the satire, scarcely any of which would reward quotation. Perhaps the best bit is that describing the degradation of the theatre, —for the "decline of the drama" is a topic for discussion as old as the playhouse itself:

Such is the drama; unbound, unrestrained,
It has rushed down to earth, and regained
The dust from which it rose; that which was art
Approaching affection, hath changed to low
And rude burlesque, and coarse buffoonery,
Which would to a wandering charlatan impart
The blush of shame; distortion and ribaldry
Are on the cheek and lip of every fostered mime,
Who famished, yet impudent, from distant clime
Adventures, dead to disgrace and shame,

These specimens must suffice to show that 'Gotham and the Gothamites' is pretty small beer, rather watery, and not likely to intoxicate with delight. It is in his notes in prose rather than in the verse of his text that the anonymous bard strives to awaken contempt for his contemporaries. But his pins are pointless, for the most part, and also headless.

Perhaps it is among the social rather than among the literary satires that we must include the 'Trollopiad; or, Travelling Gentlemen in America. A Satire. By Nil Admirari, Esq. New York: 1837.' This indignant effusion was evoked by the swift succession of British books of travel in America—Mrs. Trollope's volumes, Captain Hall's account of his wanderings, and the 'Journal' of Mrs. Fanny Kemble —books now happily as little read as this metrical retort upon them. It was in the very first number of the 'Sketch Book' that Irving warned British writers against the danger of creating ill-feeling by constant

abuse of a people who used the same language and who were likely in time to become the more important half of the race.
His good advice had the usual fate of
friendly warnings; and a succession of travellers from across the sea set forth in black
and white their casual impressions of the
people of These States, revealing sometimes a contemptuous hostility and sometimes that lordly condescension, the pleasure of which is notoriously one-sided.

The versifier of the 'Trollopiad' was
moved to wrath and called for the scourge
of the satiric poet:

POPE—GIFFORD—BYRON—what! since ye are
    fled,
Shall folly rage, and satire's self be dead?
Must he who would the warning voice repeat,
Breathe it in numbers exquisitely sweet?
And pour on dunces' ears a tide of song,
As Pope harmonious and as Dryden strong?
Oh no! my humbler muse will mark the foe,
How ill so e'er the unwonted numbers flow.
In this alone our fools are chang'd from those,—
They scrawled in verse, these haply write in prose.
They aimed at but a few their venom'd dart,

These fain would stab a nation to the heart.
Unscathed, unpunished by satiric pen,
Dulness asserts her ancient right again:
Her thousand children from her sceptre pass,
Each braying loud, proclaims himself an ASS.
The mother bids them venture and be bold,
Where Freedom reigns, and streets are paved with
    gold.
"Proceed, my sons, where TROLLOPE leads the
    way,"
"There one and all are sure to have their day."

Perhaps the most quotable passage in
this rather labored set of couplets is that
in which the British visitor is brought face
to face with the mightiest of our natural
wonders:

Arriv'd, at last, Niagara to scan,
He walks erect and feels himself a man;
Surveys the cataract with a "critic's eye,"
Resolv'd to pass no "imperfections by."
Niag'ra, wonder of the Deity,
Where God's own spirit reigns in majesty.
With sullen roar the foaming billows sweep,
A world of waters thunders o'er the steep:
The unmingled colours laugh upon the spray,
And one eternal rainbow gilds the day.
Oh! glorious God! Oh! scene surpassing all!
"True, true," quoth he, " 'tis something of a fall."
Now, shall unpunish'd such a vagrant band,

Pour like the plagues of Egypt on the land,
Eyeing each fault, to all perfection blind,
Shedding the taint of a malignant mind?

No indelible lines divide social satire from literary satire on the one side and from political on the other; but it is perhaps closer to the latter than to the former. Rather toward political than toward social satire have American wits been more often attracted. No chapters in the late Professor Moses Coit Tyler's 'Literary History of the American Revolution' are more interesting or more illuminating than those in which he considers the pungent verses of the rival bards who attacked the British cause, or who denounced the American, during the years that followed the breach with England. And it is to be noted that although the best known of all the Revolutionary satirists—Freneau especially, whom Tyler terms a "poet of hatred rather than of love"— were on the right side, yet the other party was not without its share of rhymesters, having an apt command of epigram and an ample supply of invective. For example, Dr. Jonathan Odell, who served as chaplain to the Loyalist troops, published in 1779 and 1780 four brief satires which have pith and point, and even a certain individuality of their own, although obviously imitating the method and the manner of Dryden and of Pope. There is vigor in these verses:

Was Samuel Adams to become a ghost,
Another Adams would assume his post;
Was bustling Hancock numbered with the dead,
Another full as wise might raise his head.
What if the sands of Laurens now were run,
How should we miss him—has he not a son?
Or what if Washington should close his scene,
Could none succeed him? Is there not a Greene?
Knave after knave as easy could we join,
As new emissions of the paper coin.

But nothing produced on the Tory side has half the broad humor and the pertinent wit of Trumbull's 'McFingal,' published in part in 1776 and completed in 1782. Trumbull's immediate model is obviously 'Hudibras;' but he had found his profit in

81

a study of Churchill as well as of Butler. Yet 'McFingal' is no mere imitation; or else it would have gone the swift way of all other imitations. As Professor Trent has justly remarked, Trumbull's mock epic "shows a wide and digested knowledge of the classics and of the better British poets; and while it lacks the variety and inexhaustible wit of Butler's performance, it is in many passages hardly inferior to that in pointedness and in its command of the Hudibrastic verse-form." In the minting of couplets destined to proverbial currency, Trumbull has often the felicity of Butler; and some of his sayings have had the strange fortune of ascription to the satire upon which his was modeled. For example:

> No man e'er felt the halter draw
> With good opinion of the law.

and again,

> But optics sharp it needs, I wean,
> To see what is not to be seen.

Trumbull has also not a little of Butler's

daring ingenuity in the devising of novel rhymes:

Behold! the world shall stare at new sets
Of home-made ears in Massachusetts.

After the Revolution, and before the constitution gave to the scarcely United States the firm government which the nation needed, during what the late John Fiske aptly called "the critical period of American history," Trumbull joined with others of the little group known as the "Hartford Wits" in a satire called the 'Anarchiad,' published in 1786-87, in which faction was denounced in scathing terms:

Stand forth, ye traitors, at your country's bar,
Inglorious authors of intestine war,
What countless mischiefs from their labors rise!
Pens dipped in gall, and lips inspired with lies!
Ye sires of ruin, prime detested cause
Of bankrupt faith, annihilated laws,
Of selfish systems, jealous, local schemes,
And unvoiced empire lost in empty dreams;
Your names, expanding with your growing crime,
Shall float disgustful down the stream of time;
Each future age applaud the avenging song,
An outraged nature vindicate the wrong.

83

All things considered, the most amusing political effort in this field between the Revolution and the War of 1812, was the 'Embargo; or, Sketches of the Times. A Satire by a Youth of Thirteen; Boston, 1808. Printed for the purchasers.' This met with so much success that it was issued in a second edition in the following year. The youth of thirteen survived to be the boy of eighteen, who wrote 'Thanatopsis,' and who was the earliest American poet to transmute into his verse the beauty of nature here in America. Bryant lived to be not a little annoyed when he was reminded of his youthful indiscretion, for with the flight of time he outgrew the political opinions he had taken over from his father and from his father's Federalist friends. Bryant came to have a high regard for the character and for the public services and even for most of the political theories of the Jefferson whom the youth of thirteen had ignorantly berated:

And thou the scorn of every patriot's name
Thy country's ruin and thy council's shame!
Poor servile thing! derision of the brave!
Who erst from Tarleton fled to Carter's Cave;
Thou who when menaced by perfidious Gaul,
Did'st prostrate to her whisker'd minions fall;
And when our cash her empty bags supplied
Did'st meanly strive the foul disgrace to hide;
Go, wretch, resign the Presidential chair,
Disclose thy secret measures, foul or fair.
Go search with curious eye for horrid frogs
Mid the wild wastes of Louisianian bogs;
Or where the Ohio rolls his turbid stream,
Dig for huge bones, thy glory and thy theme.
Go scan, Philosophist, thy Sally's charms,
And sink supinely in her sable arms;
But quit to abler hands the helm of State.

Beyond all question the best American
political satire is Lowell's 'Biglow Papers,'
the first series being written during the
Mexican War and the second during the
Civil War. Although either series may
seem fragmentary, each has a real unity
of its own; the aim and intent is ever the
same. And the unforgettable figure of
Hosea Biglow dominates both sets of
satiric lyrics. Lowell was at once a Puri-

tan by descent, a poet by gift of nature,
and a wit by stroke of fate; and in the
'Biglow Papers' we have revealed the Puritan poet who could not help being witty.
He could not help preaching, for as he
said "all New England was a meeting-
house" when he was young; and a satirist
must be a preacher in his own way. He
had enlisted for the war, and he was ever
fighting the good fight. His heart was
in his cause; and his desire to help it along,
made him conquer the indolence which so
often prevented his doing his best as a
poet. Lowell tended to improvise, to
brood long over a theme, and then to pour
out his lines in a sudden burst of inspiration,
not always taking the trouble afterward to
revise and to refine, to finish and to polish,
and to make the most of his genius. It
is this which accounts for the inequality
of his odes. But when he was at work on
the 'Biglow Papers' he wanted to bring
his message home, and he waited until he
had found a taking rhythm and a refrain

that would sing itself into the memory.
And so we cannot forget, even if we would,
that

> John P
> Robinson, he
> Sez he won't vote for Guvnor B.

and that

> Ole Uncle S, sez he, "I guess
> It is a fact," sez he,
> "The surest plan to make a man
> Is, think him so, J. B.
> Ez much ez you or me!"

Here, as so often in the history of all
the arts, we see that the artist has profited
by his willingness to take time and trouble,
and by his honesty in resolutely grappling
with difficulty. The two refrains quoted
above are, one of them from the first series,
and the other from the second; and this
reminds us that Lowell succeeded as well
the second time he chose Hosea Biglow
for his mouthpiece, as he did the first time,
although in literature a sequel is generally

a feeble thing, a faint imitation of its more vigorous elder brother. The motive that impelled the poet was even stronger during the Civil War than it had been fifteen years earlier; and the wit was no less keen nor the humor less contagious. That Heaven is on the side of the heaviest battalions, is an old saying, and almost equally venerable is the belief that it is generally the losing cause which inspires the poet and also the satirist. Certainly Aristophanes seems to us now to have been on the wrong side in the 'Clouds' and in the 'Knights;' and Butler in his 'Hudibras' was making fun of the stern Puritan who had enough iron in his blood to win the victory at last. But here in the United States we have been more fortunate. Clever as were some of the Tory wits, the one satire of the Revolution which can still be read with pleasure, is the 'McFingal' of the more patriotic Trumbull; and in the Civil War nothing produced in the South can withstand comparison with the 'Biglow Papers.'

In the third division of satire, the purely literary, we find Lowell again the chief figure with the 'Fable for Critics,' published in 1848, the same year that he sent forth the first series of the 'Biglow Papers' and also the more purely poetic 'Vision of Sir Launfal.' But the 'Fable for Critics' was preceded by another formal and elaborate attempt at literary satire, called 'Truth,' published in 1832; and it was followed by yet another entitled 'Parnassus in Pillory,' issued in 1851. Neither of these attains to the level of Lowell's brilliant skit; and they soon faded out of remembrance. Yet each of them has an interest of its own, and calls for cursory consideration here.

'Truth, a Gift for Scribblers,' by William J. Snelling, seems to have achieved a certain success, sufficient at least to cause it to be reprinted,—since it is a second edition "with additions and emendations" that I now have before me. Mr. Snelling tells us how he heard

         a voice that cries, "Lift up thine hand
Against the legions of this locust band;
Let brain-sick youths the wholesome scourge endure;
Their case is urgent. Spare not! Kill or cure!
Hang, hang them up, like smelts upon a string,
And o'er their books a *requiescat* sing:
Arise!—convince thy country of her shame;
Rise, ere her genius be no more a name!

Rous'd by the call of Duty, I obey;
I draw the sword, and fling the sheath away.

And with the blade thus drawn, Mr.
Snelling runs amuck amid the minor American authors of his day, hewing and hacking, and yet not revealing any gift of swordsmanship which would let him wound with a sharp epithet or kill with a piercing couplet. Here is a sample of his execution wrought upon the once-popular N. P. Willis:

Muse, shall we not a few brief lines afford
To give poor Natty P.—his meet reward?
What has he done to be despised by all
Within whose hands his harmless scribblings fall?
Why, as in band-box trim, he walks the streets,
Turns up the nose of every man he meets,
As if it scented carrion? Why, of late,
Do all the critics claw his shallow pate?

From a note in this second edition, it appears that Willis had retorted with an unworthy attempt at an epigram, to which Snelling retaliated with three several efforts of his own, not quite so gross as Willis's, but far feebler. A man of taste often finds it needful to hold his nose as he reads the lines of the less inspired satirists; and as to the reasons for this he had best hold his tongue forever after. Far more agreeable is it to quote Snelling's eulogy of Fitz-Greene Halleck, whose fame is now sadly faded:

> Dear Halleck, wither'd be the hands that dare
> One laurel from thy nobler brow to tear;
> Accept the tribute of a muse inclin'd
> To bow to nothing, save the power of mind.
> Bard of Bozzaris, shall thy native shore
> List to thy harp and mellow voice no more?
> Shall we, with skill like thine so near at hand,
> Import our music from a foreign land?
> While *Mirror* Morris chants in whimpering note,
> And croaking Dana strains his screech-owl throat;
> While crazy Neal to metre shakes his chains,
> And fools are found to listen to his strains,
> Wilt thou be silent? Wake, O Halleck, wake!

Thine and thy country's honor are at stake;
Wake, and redeem the pledge; thy vantage keep;
While Paulding wakes and writes, shall Halleck
sleep?

Snelling has words of praise also for
Bryant; but he falls foul of Whittier; and
he delights in abuse of the first efforts of
the native American dramatists, especially
deriding Stone, who had just devised 'Meta-
mora' for the robust talents of Edwin
Forrest.

It was not Snelling's forgotten 'Truth'
which evoked the next and the best of
American literary satires—the only one
indeed which has a permanent value. The
immediate cause of the 'Fable for Critics'
seems to have been Leigh Hunt's 'Feast
of the Poets,' although the influence of
Goldsmith's 'Retaliation' is also apparent.
Indeed, it is only in 'Retaliation' that we
can find a gallery of lightly limned contemporary portraits worthy of comparison with
the collection contained in the 'Fable.' Perfect as is Goldsmith's portrayal of Burke

and Reynolds and Garrick, it is not finer or truer than Lowell's depicting of Irving or of Cooper, or than the companion pictures of Emerson and Carlyle. In his affectionate essay on Dryden, Lowell quotes Dryden's assertion that Chaucer was "a perpetual fountain of good sense," only to suggest that the phrase may be applied to Dryden himself; it fits the American critic-poet almost as well as the British poet-critic. Half a century is it since Lowell narrated his 'Fable;' and even at this late date his criticism seems to us to be rarely at fault.

Not only did he set forth fifty years ago an opinion of his contemporaries anticipating the judgment of the twentieth century, but he chose with unerring instinct the writers whom it was worth while to consider. Here is the weak spot of most literary satires; they deal with the dead already; they slay the petty critics and minor poets certain to die of their own accord, and to be forgotten in a flash. This is what makes the 'Dunciad' unreadable nowadays except by indefatigable students of the period. Pope gratified his spite against the criticasters and the poetasters, victims really unworthy of his wit; and as a result his lines are now read only by those attracted by his fame. His theme is not to-day tempting to the general reader, and the resolute perusal of the 'Dunciad' demands both courage and endurance. But the 'Fable for Critics' is alluring not only to admirers of Lowell, but to all having an interest in the group of American men of letters who adorned the middle of the nine-teenth century.

Of course there are those who hold that the machinery of the fable creaks a little, that the rattling rhymes run away with the lyrist more than once, that the rhythm is somewhat rugged now and again, that the puns are not always as expensive as they might be, that there are other blemishes to be detected by a severe critic. But ever against these trifling defects set the brilliant truth of the characters of Hawthorne and Holmes and Whittier. Consider, for example, the cleverness of the portrait of Poe, and note that the sketch is really just, in spite of the crackling of epigram:

There comes Poe, with his raven, like Barnaby Rudge,
Three fifths of him genius and two fifths sheer. fudge,
Who talks like a book of iambs and pentameters,
In a way to make people of common sense damn metres,
Who has written some things quite the best of their kind,
But the heart somehow seems all squeezed out by the mind, . . .

And the sketch of Bryant, with all the ingenuity of its punning and all the artificiality of its rhyming, is not a caricature but a true portrait:

There is Bryant, as quiet, as cool, and as dignified,
As a smooth, silent iceberg, that never is ignified,
Save when the reflection 'tis kindled o' nights
With a semblance of flame by the chill Northern Lights.
He may rank (Griswold says so) first bard of your nation

(There's no doubt that he stands in supreme ice-
olation),
Your topmost Parnassus he may set his heel on,
But no warm applauses come, peal following peal
on,—
He's too smooth and too polished to hang any zeal
on:
Unqualified merits, I'll grant, if you choose, he has
'em,
But he lacks the one merit of kindling enthusiasm;
If he stir you at all, it is just, on my soul,
Like being stirred up with the very North Pole.

He is very nice reading in summer, but *inter
Nos,* we don't want *extra* freezing in winter;
Take him up in the depth of July, my advice is,
When you feel an Egyptian devotion to ices.
But, deduct all you can, there's enough that's right
good in him,
He has a true soul for field, river, and wood in him;
And his heart, in the midst of brick walls, or
where'er it is,
Glows, softens, and thrills with the tenderest chari-
ties.

If a properly annotated edition of the
'Fable for Critics' should ever be published,
—and it would be warmly welcomed by all
students of American literature—the editor
will call attention to Lowell's own opinion

of this passage, expressed in one of his letters. He declared that his criticism of
Bryant was "funny and as fair as I could
make it, immitigably just. Indeed, I have
endeavored to be so in all." The friend
to whom he was writing had informed
Lowell that Bryant seemed to think that
the younger poet had been borrowing from
him. It is to this that Lowell was referring when he continued, "I am glad I did
Bryant before I got your letter . . . .
I steal from him indeed! If he knew me he
would not say so. When I steal I shall
go to a specie-vault, not to a till."

Although he was dealing solely with the
literature of his own country, Lowell had
ever a cosmopolitan point of view, while
still keeping his feet firm on his native soil.
He was never either provincial in self-asser-
tion or colonial in self-abasement. No one
had higher ideals for America; and no one
was prompter to see the absurdity of hasty
assertions that these ideals had already been
attained. He refused resolutely to see a

Swan of Avon in any of our wild geese.
He laughed to scorn the suggestion that
we ought to have great poets of our own
merely because of the vastness of the country. He had a healthy detestation of that
confession of inferiority which consists in
calling Irving the "American Goldsmith,"
and Cooper the "American Scott." It was
this youthful foible—feebler now than it
was when the 'Fable' was written, but not
yet quite dead—that Lowell girded against
in one of his most brilliant passages:

By the way, 'tis a fact that displays what profusions
Of all kinds of greatness bless free institutions,
That while the Old World has produced barely eight
Of such poets as all men agree to call great,
And of other great characters hardly a score
(One might safely say less than that rather than
    more),
With you every year a whole crop is begotten,
They're as much of a staple as corn is, or cotton;
Why, there's scarcely a huddle of log-huts and
    shanties
That has not brought forth its own Miltons and
    Dantes;
I myself know ten Byrons, one Coleridge, three
    Shelleys,

Two Raphaels, six Titians, (I think) one Apelles,
Leonardos and Rubenses plenty as lichens,
One (but that one is plenty) American Dickens,
A whole flock of Lambs, any number of Tennysons,—
In short, if a man has the luck to have any sons,
He may feel pretty certain that one out of twain
Will be some very great person over again.

This same foible we find animadverted upon again in 'Parnassus in Pillory. A Satire. By Motley Manners, Esquire. New York: 1851.' The anonymous bard, now known to be A. J. H. Duganne, bemoaned the sad plight of his own country:

Oh, hapless land of mine! whose country-presses
Labor with poets and with poetesses;
Where Helicon is quaffed like beer at table,
And Pegasus is "hitched" in every stable;
Where each smart dunce presumes to print a journal,
And every journalist is dubbed a "colonel;"
Where love-sick girls on chalk and water thrive,
And prove, by singing, they're unfit to wive;
Where Gray might Miltons by the score compute—
"Inglorious" all, but, ah! by no means "mute."

And there is sense as well as vigor in his denunciation of that colonial attitude

of so many Americans in the days before
the Civil War had made us somewhat less
self-conscious:

The British critics—be it to their glory,
When they abuse us, do it *con amore;*
There's no half-way about your bulldog pure,
And there's no nonsense with your "Scotch reviewer."
Heaven knows how often we've been whipped like
    curs,
By those to whom we've knelt as worshippers;
Heaven only knows how oft, like froward chitlings,
Our authors have been snubbed by British witlings;
Our mountains ranked as mole-hills—our immense
And awful forests styled "Virginny fence;"
Our virtues all but damned with faintest praise,
And our faults blazoned to the widest gaze!
I find no fault with them—they praise us rarely;
As for abuse—we're open to it fairly;
But faith, it galls me, and I'll not deny it,
To mark our own most deferential quiet;
To note the whining, deprecative air
With which we beg for praise, or censure bear;
Shrink back in terror if our gifts they spurn,
And if they smite one cheek, the other turn;—
Begging that they'll excuse a patient dunce,
Who, if he could, would offer both at once.

Perhaps as good as any of the portraits
in 'Parnassus in Pillory' is this of Lowell:

O, LOWELL! now sententious—now most wordy—
Thy harp Cremona half—half hurdy-gurdy;
Wouldst thou arise, and climb the steeps of heaven?
Sandals and staff are for thy journey given;
Wouldst thou embrace the poet-preacher's lot?
Nor purse nor scrip will lift thy steps a jot!
Forth on the highways of the general mind,
Thy soul must walk, in oneness with mankind.
Thou hast done well, but thou canst yet do better,
And winning credit, make the world thy debtor;
Pour out thy heart—albeit with flaws and fractures:
Give us thyself—no "Lowell manufactures."

The past fifty years have not called forth
another formal satire of contemporary literature, although the need is as acute now
as it ever was, and although the public relish
for ill-natured remarks is as keen as ever.
Probably one reason why the longer satire
in verse does not make its appearance is
because the immense multiplication of peri-
odicals, weekly and monthly, affords to the
intending satirist a chance to shoot his
shafts one by one in the papers without
having to save them up for discharge in a
volley and in a volume. Thus it was that
the late H. C. Bunner—a cordial lover of

poetry, with a trained craftsman's appreciation of technic, with a keen sense of humor and with a singular gift of parody, —put forth his satires week by week in the paper he had conducted with prosperity. He evoked the figure of V. Hugo Dusenbury, a professional poet, understanding all branches of the business, and ready to supply any kind of verse on demand, in quantities to suit the customer. If some future enthusiast shall ransack the files of *Puck* to edit the 'Life and Literary Remains of V. Hugo Dusenbury,' a younger generation of readers will be enabled to make the acquaintance of an original character sketched with journalistic breadth and freedom, but not really caricatured beyond resemblance. And the poems which this professional poet produced by request and to meet the market, are parodies, most of them, or rather sympathetic imitations, satiric enough at times, appreciative often, and never malignant.

(1904).

VI

AMERICAN EPIGRAMS

IN the elaborate and scholarly introduction to Mr. Dodd's comprehensive collection of the 'Epigrammatists' may be found an amusing
illustration of the inability of a man
of letters to accept the obvious fact that
language is made in the street as well
as in the study, and that in common usage
the meaning of a word may broaden despite the utmost endeavor of precisians to
keep it restricted. A word has the meaning which the plain people give it; and the
trained and careful student of speech must
kick in vain against the modifications of
meaning which take place in spite of his
protests. Mr. Dodd insists that the word
epigram, being taken over from the Greek,
must preserve in English exactly the sig-

nificance that it had in the language from which we have derived it. In Greek *epigram, epigraph* and *epitaph* have substantially the same meaning; and all three words were applied to brief lyrics elevated in thought and having the lapidary concision of an inscription. In Latin, Martial debased the epigram; and in his hands it is a metrical phrasing of an ingenious point or of a keen retort. It is Martial whom the epigrammatists of the modern languages have taken as their master; and therefore in English the primary meaning of epigram is no longer a tiny lyric, lofty in sentiment, and graceful in phrasing; it is more an ingeniously turned witticism adroitly rhymed.

Landor, who might almost be called a belated Athenian, declared that one of his own brief pieces "resembles not those ridiculous quibbles which the English in particular call epigrams, but rather . . . those exquisite *eidyllia*, which are modestly called epigrams by the Greeks." And

Mr. Dodd insists again and again that there is no such thing as an epigram unless it follows the Greek model. That the English word *epigram* still retains this special meaning may perhaps be admitted, but this is no longer its only meaning,— or even its accepted meaning; and any writer who uses language as a means of communicating his thought to the main body of his readers, and who desires to be understood by them, will do well to find some other word to describe the epigram of the purest Greek type, and will accept the fact that in ordinary every-day English epigram now evokes the idea of a brilliant witticism. The common usage of the word nowadays is revealed by the frequent description of the dialogue of Congreve and Sheridan as epigrammatic.

It is not that English literature is deficient in brief poems having the special qualities that we find in the Greek epigram. Even in the 'Greek Anthology' it would be difficult to discover a poem more delicately felicitous than the epitaph on the Countess of Pembroke:

> Underneath this sable hearse
> Lies the subject of all verse,
> Sidney's sister, Pembroke's mother;
> Death, ere thou hast slain another
> Learn'd and fair and good as she
> Time shall throw a dart at thee.

And it would not be an arduous task to collect other instances where the poets of our language have rivalled the austere perfection of the Greek. But none the less has *epigram* come to indicate to us not a votive tablet but a sparkling retort. Perhaps the best definition of what we moderns understand by an epigram is contained in one which is ascribed by some to an unknown Latin writer and by others to the Spanish fabulist, Yriarte:

> The qualities all in a bee that we meet,
> In an epigram never should fail;
> The body should always be little and sweet,
> And a sting should be felt in its tail.

This is at once a description and an illustration; and to be set by the side of it is

an even terser attempt by an anonymous
wit:

> What is an epigram? a dwarfish whole,
> Its body brevity, and wit its soul.

One of these is Latin or Spanish and the
other is British; and to them may be added
a third by an American, Mr. George
Birdseye:

> The diamond's virtues well might grace
>   The epigram, and both excel
> In brilliancy in smallest space,
>   And power to cut, as well.

Although we no longer demand in an
epigram the ancient ingenuity of sentiment,
preferring the modern wit that seeks to
surprise, we ought not to debase the standard and to accept as a true epigram merely
a rhymed pun or a versified anecdote. Mr.
Dodd has quoted, from the preface of a
collection published in London in 1735,
a protest against these inexpressive rhymes,
which hope to pass themselves off for epigrams: "We have already observed what
a gay conceit, or a good sentence, will some-

times serve for points: but what else? Nothing so properly as what can truly be called wit; no jingle of words, pun, quibble, conundrum, mixed wit, or false wit, ought ever to be used, though they have all very often appeared in this kind of poetry."

A rhymed pun, it is true, may sometimes have a certain unexpected felicity which is its own excuse for being. Here is a couplet by an American rhymester—who in these papers must remain anonymous—on the 'Danse Macabre' of M. Saint-Saëns:

> This dance of death, which sounds so musically,
> Was sure intended for the *corpse de ballet*.

And this couplet may be matched by a quatrain, written by Mrs. Lydia Maria Child a half century earlier when a young friend of hers named Nathaniel Deering moved his residence to the town of Canaan:

> Whoever weds the young lawyer at C.
>   Will surely have prospects most cheering,
> For what must his person and intellect be,
>   When even his name is "N. Deering?"

Even the versified anecdote may attain the requisite pithiness of the true epigram as we now understand the term; and perhaps as good an example as any that might be chosen is John Boyle O'Reilly's on the 'Lure':

"What bait do you use," said a saint to the devil,
  "When you fish where the souls of men abound?"
"Well, for special tastes," said the king of evil,
  "Gold and fame are the best I've found."
"But for general use?" asked the saint. "Ah, then,"
Said the demon, "I angle for man, not men,
        And a thing I hate,
        Is to change my bait,
So I fish with a woman the whole year round."

But the mere pun in rhyme and the bare anecdote in verse, frequent as they both are, belong to an inferior order of effort. The true epigram is not often based on a pun, which has been called the lowest form of wit—because, as a punster explained, it is the foundation of all wit. And the true epigram does not need to be sustained by a story. The true epigram indeed relies on its own wit and it flies aloft on the

twin wings of buoyancy and brilliancy—
and here is its close resemblance to familiar
verse, as Cowper called it, to *vers de
société*, as it is more often entitled.

It is a curious fact that Mr. Dodd's
collection of epigrams, which he sought to
make as comprehensive as possible and
which must contain two or three thousand
specimens from almost every literature
ancient and modern, does not include a
single exan.ple by an American author.
And it is almost equally curious that no
American editor has as yet attempted to
gather together an adequate representation
of the epigrams of American authorship.
This species of poetry seems to call for
wit rather than humor; and the American
gift is rather for humor than for wit. And
yet there is no lack of epigrams of American authorship, of varying merit, no doubt,
but permitting a selection not unworthy
of comparison with what has been done
of late years, either by our kin across the
sea in Great Britain, or by the satiric poets

of France. Many of the turning points of American history have found record in the couplets and quatrains of the American epigrammatists.

For example, it happened that the motto on the colors of the Hessians who were defeated at Trenton was *Nescit Pericula*, and as their behavior on this occasion was not over-valiant, an American carelessly rhymed this uncomplimentary quatrain:

The man who submits without striking a blow,
May be said in a sense no danger to know:
I pray then, what harm, by the humble submission,
At Trenton was done by the standard of Hessian.

Another Revolutionary epigram was probably written by David Edwards not long after the event it commemorates, Burgoyne's surrender:

Burgoyne, alas, unknowing future fates,
Could force his way through woods, but not through
    Gates.

The neatness of the pun was probably appreciated by the debonair British general whose own wit was displayed in the comedy of the 'Heiress,' which held the stage for several years in England. It was the surrender of Burgoyne which encouraged the French to come to our aid; and it was the French alliance which brought more swiftly the independence of this country and the establishment of a stable government on the basis of human equality. The most important implement of any such government must be the ballot; and no one attempting to collect the most striking of American epigrams could afford to omit the quatrain of the Reverend John Pierpont on the 'Ballot':

> A weapon that comes down as still
> As snowflakes fall upon the sod;
> But executes a freeman's will,
> As lightning does the will of God.

The Civil War brought forth a fruitage of epigrams as abundant as that of the Revolution; and of these one of the earliest was written when Admiral Foote was engaged in clearing the Mississippi:

The rebels say, in boasting way,
They'll every inch of ground dispute;
A brag, indeed, we'll better heed
Whenever they withstand one Foote.

The mock epitaph has always been a favorite form of epigram, and sometimes a real epitaph may have an epigrammatic flavor. When the Union troops withdrew after one of the battles in front of Richmond, a Confederate soldier is said to have buried a dead opponent and to have written on a shingle stuck at the head of the grave these rather grewsome lines:

The Yankee hosts with blood-stained hands
Came southward to divide our lands.
This narrow and contracted spot
Is all that this poor Yankee got.

After the capture of the President of the Confederacy, Charles G. Halpine, who was better known as "Miles O'Reilly," put into circulation a fragment of verse which he called 'An Old Maxim Reversed':

Et arma cedunt toga,
Said a Roman of renown:
When the din of war is over,
Arms yield unto the gown.

But this motto Jeff reverses:
For, arrayed in female charms,
When the din of war is over,
In his gown he yields to arms.

After the war came the dread period of Reconstruction, followed by the sorrowful days of brutal ring rule in New York and in Boston. It was probably Tweed of New York, whose brazen career evoked from Lowell a biting couplet on the 'Boss':

Skilled to pull wires, he baffles Nature's hope,
Who sure intended him to stretch a rope.

And it was probably Butler of Massachusetts who called forth a scorching quatrain which Lowell liked enough to include in his latest volume of verse, and which he termed a 'Misconception':

B. taught by Pope to do his good by stealth,
 'Twixt participle and noun no difference feeling;
In office placed to serve the Commonwealth,
 Does himself all the good he can by stealing.

During the long labors of the American Copyright League to secure such an amendment to our laws which would give foreign authors an honest reward for their work while relieving American writers from an enforced competition with stolen goods, Lowell served as President, and he lived only a few months after the law went into effect which he had helped to pass. To aid in arousing the popular conscience against the sin of literary piracy he wrote an epigram, which the League immediately took for its motto:

> In vain we call old notions fudge,
> And bend our conscience to our dealing;
> The ten commandments will not budge,
> And stealing *will* continue stealing.

Another epigram of Lowell's, written on his sixty-eighth birthday, falls within the later definition of the epigram, while it lies at ease also within the earlier definition, which insists rather on a serenity such as we look for in a Greek inscription:

> As life runs on, the road grows strange
> With faces new, and near the end
> The milestones into headstones change,
> 'Neath everyone a friend.

With this austere quatrain of Lowell's may be contrasted another by Emerson, written originally in an album:

> The man who has a thousand friends
> Has not a friend to spare;
> But he who has one enemy
> Will meet him everywhere.

In one of his letters Lowell describes a dull dinner in London with a dozen and a half speakers droning away till long after midnight, the only brilliant exception being Sir Frederick Bramwell, who was called upon very late to respond to Applied Science, and who said that "at this time of night the only illustration of the toast I can think of would be the application of the domestic safety-match to the bed-room candle." Whereupon Lowell promptly handed him this impromptu, scribbled on a card:

> Oh, brief Sir Frederick, might the others catch
> Your happy science,—and supply your match!

This couplet of Lowell's improvised at

a dinner may be followed by a quatrain of Longfellow's improvised in an inn-album. At the Sign of the Raven in Zürich Longfellow was overcharged for unsatisfactory accommodation; and he contributed to the landlord's book these four lines of warning to other travellers:

> Beware of the Raven of Zürich,
> 'Tis a bird of omen ill,
> With an ugly, unclean nest
> And a very, very long bill.

Another of Longfellow's playful and careless quatrains has also been preserved:

> When you ask one friend to dine,
> Give him your best wine!
> When you ask two,
> The second best will do!

It is to Martial that we can trace the turning aside of the epigram from sentiment to wit; and in his hands the epigram may pierce like the keenest of rapiers or it may batter like a brutal bludgeon. He is willing to employ either weapon against the sex he was at once pursuing and abusing. Woman, indeed, has always been a shining mark for the hurtling shafts of the epigrammatists of all countries. It was Fitz-Greene Halleck, who adapted from Goethe a sarcastic quatrain, which he called 'Honor to Woman':

All honor to Woman, the Sweetheart, the Wife,
  The delight of our homesteads by night and by day,
The darling who never does harm in her life,—
  Except when determined to have her own way.

Several of the epigrams of John G. Saxe are directed against feminine failings. Just now, when so many women affect to be mannish, there is perhaps a certain pertinence in the pair of couplets he called a 'Dilemma':

"Whenever I marry," says masculine Ann,
"I must really insist upon wedding a man!"
But what if the man (for men are but human)
Should be equally nice about wedding a woman?

Another of Saxe's is rather a rhymed retort than a true epigram; and it has the further disadvantage of recalling a little too closely one of the cleverest repartees in the 'School for Scandal.' Yet it is so neatly turned that it deserves quotation here. It is called 'Too Candid by Half':

As Tom and his wife were discoursing one day
Of their several faults in a bantering way,
   Said she: "Though my wit you disparage,
I'm sure, my dear husband, our friends will attest
This much, at the least, that my judgment is best."
   Quoth Tom, "So they said at our marriage."

One of the most striking epigrams about women was written by a woman—the late Anne Reeve Aldrich, who gave her lines the enigmatic title, 'Suppose':

How sad if, by some strange new law,
   All kisses scarred!
For she who is most beautiful
   Would be most marred.
And we might be surprised to see
   Some lovely wife
Smooth-visaged, while a seeming prude
   Was marked for life.

Another woman, Miss Mary Ainge De

Vere, has put a certain feminine subtlety into her 'Friend and Lover':

> When Psyche's friend becomes her lover,
> How sweetly these conditions blend!
> But, oh, what anguish to discover
> Her lover has become—her friend!

But it was a man, Mr. Gordon Campbell, who phrased an opinion more masculine in the quatrain which he termed 'My Idol':

> My idol fell down and was utterly broken,
> The fragments of stone lay all scattered apart;
> And I picked up the hardest to keep as a token—
> Her heart.

It was a man again, Mr. W. D. Howells, who wrote this quatrain on 'A Sarcastic Woman':

> Her mouth is a honey-blossom,
> No doubt, as the poet sings;
> But within her lips, the petals,
> Lurks a cruel bee, that stings.

And another man, the sculptor-poet, W. W. Story, rhymed these lines on 'Persica':

> Oh, Persica, Persica, pale and fair,
> With a ripe blush on your cheek,
> How pretty—how very pretty you are,
> Until you begin to speak!

As for a heart and soul, my dear,
You have not enough to sin;
Outside so fair, like a peach you are,
With a stone for a heart within.

And it was a third man, Mr. George Birdseye, who ventured upon the attempt to elucidate the wiles of a 'Coquette':

Her pleasure is in lovers coy;
When hers, she gives them not a thought;
But, like the angler, takes more joy
In fishing than in fishes caught.

The same title served Mr. Thomas Bailey Aldrich for a most pungent and imaginative accusation against a type of woman not unfeminine:

Or light or dark, or short or tall,
She sets a spring to snare them all;
All's one to her;—above her fan
She'd make sweet eyes at Caliban.

And to Mr. Walter Learned we are indebted for one of the pleasantest of the many glancing shafts which have enlivened the merry war between the sexes. He has chosen to call it 'Humility':

You say, when I kissed you, you are sure I must quite
Have forgotten myself. So I did; you are right.
No, I'm not such an egotist, dear, it is true,
As to think of myself when I'm looking at you.

The relation between literature and life is so close that there is no need to discuss which of these it was Mr. Aldrich had in mind when he penned his quatrain on 'Masks':

Black Tragedy lets slip her grim disguise
And shows you laughing lips and roguish eyes;
But when, unmasked, gay Comedy appears,
How wan her cheeks are, and what heavy tears!

But it is easy to guess that it was the rude but powerful poems of Walt Whitman that Mr. Aldrich was criticizing when he wrote his lines, 'On Reading—'

Great thoughts in crude, unshapely verse set forth
    Lose half their preciousness and ever must.
    Unless the diamond with its own rich dust
Be cut and polished, it seems little worth.

Indeed, authors have taken each other for the targets of their satire quite as frequently as they have chosen to gird at the other sex. Mr. Richard Watson Gilder packed his scorn of an empty rhymester into a terse quatrain, which he entitled 'Wanted, A Theme':

"Give me a theme," the little poet cried—
  "And I will do my part."
" 'Tis not a theme you need," the world replied;
  "You need a heart."

And the same lyrist gave another turn to almost the same thought in the cutting lines of his 'Strephon and Sardon':

"Young Strephon wears his heart upon his sleeve,"
  Thus Sardon spoke, with scoffing air;
Perhaps 'twas envy made the gray-beard grieve—
  For Sardon never had a heart to wear.

Mr. J. T. Trowbridge in his autobiography preserves for us the six lines of rhyme evoked from him by the short-range contemplation of the curious characteristics of Bronson Alcott:

Do you care to meet Alcott? His mind is a mirror,
Reflecting the unspoken thought of his hearer:
To the great he is great; to the fool he's a fool:
In the world's dreary desert a crystalline pool,
Where a lion looks in and a lion appears;
But an ass will see only his own ass's ears.

When water was first brought into Boston there was much discussion as to the healthfulness of the conduits through which it was conveyed; and this evoked from Longfellow these pungent rhymes:

> Cochituate water, it is said,
> Though introduced in pipes of lead,
>   Will not prove deleterious;
> But if the stream of Helicon
> Through leaden pipes is made to run,
>   ˙ The effect is very serious.

An undergraduate rhymester of Columbia, Mr. Russell H. Loines, has voiced a feeling which many another reader of ephemeral verse will swiftly recognize. He was writing 'On a Magazine Sonnet':

> "Scorn not the sonnet," though its strength be sapped,
>   Nor say malignant its inventor blundered;
> The corpse that here in fourteen lines is wrapped
>   Had otherwise been covered with a hundred.

Mr. Stedman has told us that no other American poets have been so frequently discussed in print as Whitman and Poe. Mr. Aldrich's epigram, which we may assume to have Whitman for its theme,

has already been quoted; and there are not
a few epigrams on Poe, although no one
of them rivals the polish and the point of
Mr. Aldrich's. There is, however, one
worthy of quotation, one launched by
Father Tabb against 'Poe's Critics':

> A certain tyrant, to disgrace
> The more a rebel's resting place,
> Compelled the people every one
> To hurl, in passing there, a stone,
> Which done, behold, the pile became
> A monument to keep the name.
>
> And thus it is with Edgar Poe;
> Each passing critic has his throw,
> Nor sees, defeating his intent,
> How lofty grows the monument.

Another there is, not against Poe or
against his critics either, but having as its
theme a pretentious biography of the American poet by a British writer:

> An Englishman, Ingram, has written Poe's life;
> We recall, as we slowly toil through it,
> How keenly Poe wielded the critical knife,
> And we wish he were here to review it.

Not quite so concise, and rather more

vigorous in expression, are a dozen lines by the late Richard Henry Stoddard, in which he dwelt on the widespread success of the author of 'Proverbial Philosophy':

Hail to Martin Farquhar Tupper!
Who, when he bestrides the crupper
Of Pegasus, gets the upper
Hand of poets more renowned;
Everywhere his works are found,
In poor men's huts, rich men's pavilions,
Sold by thousands, sold by millions;
Suited to all times and latitudes,
By the everlasting platitudes
Spread for breakfast, dinner, supper,
Hail to Martin Farquhar Tupper!

When a contributor to a long-forgotten literary weekly, the *Round Table,* chanced to refer disparagingly to a certain essay by Richard Grant White, that lively but sensitive essayist retorted at once with these brisk couplets:

Some knight of King Arthur's, Sir Void or Sir Null,
Swears a trifle I wrote is respectably dull.
He is honest for once through his weakness of wit,
And he censures a fault that he does not commit;
For he shows by example—proof quite unrejectable—
That a man may be dull *without* being respectable.

During one of the more heated periods of the absurd and unending discussion of the foolish suggestion that the plays of Shakspere were in reality written by Bacon, the late T. W. Parsons, best known as a devout student of Dante, ventured into the arena with these convincing lines:

Shakspere! whoever thou mayst prove to be,
God save the Bacon that men find in thee!
If that philosopher, though bright and wise,
Those lofty labors did in truth devise,
Then it must follow, as the night the day,
That 'Hamlet,' 'Lear,' 'Macbeth,' and each great play
That certifies nobility of mind,
Was written by the "meanest of mankind."

And to this must be adjoined the suggestive quatrain of Mr. Aldrich, which he has wittily entitled 'Points of View':

Bonnet in hand, obsequious and discreet,
The butcher that served Shakspere with his meat
Doubtless esteemed him little, as a man
Who knew not how the market prices ran.

Another admirable quatrain of Mr. Aldrich's expresses his wholesome dissatisfaction with the bards of despair; this is the epigram which he terms 'Pessimistic Poets':

I little read those poets who have made
A noble art a pessimistic trade,
And trained their Pegasus to draw a hearse
Through endless avenues of drooping verse.

Books as well as belles were sometimes the target for the arrows of Saxe's easy wit; and one of his prettily-phrased epigrams is entitled *'Lucas a non'*:

You'll oft find in books, rather ancient than recent,
A gap in the page marked *"cetera desunt,"*
By which you may commonly take it for granted
The passage is wanting—without being wanted;
And may borrow, besides a significant hint
That *desunt* means simply not decent to print.

Oliver Wendell Holmes was ever a facile and felicitous writer of occasional verse; and he was a master of *vers de société* with its subtly blended sentiment and humor; but he was rarely willing to limit himself within the narrow boundaries of the epigram. Indeed, there is apparently only one of his shorter poems which falls fairly within the definition. This is the amusing example of fanciful imagination which he chose to call 'Cacœthes Scribendi':

If all the trees in all the woods were men;
And each and every blade of grass a pen;
If every leaf on every shrub and tree
Turned to a sheet of foolscap; every sea
Were changed to ink, and all the earth's living tribes
Had nothing else to do but act as scribes,
And for ten thousand ages, day and night,
The human race should write, and write and write,
Till all the pens and paper were used up,
And the huge inkstand was an empty cup,
Still would the scribblers clustered round its brink
Call for more pens, more paper, and more ink.

There are many epigrammatic stanzas scattered through Holmes's occasional verses; but this is perhaps the only specimen of his effort in the briefer form with the severe unity of theme which the true epigram insists upon. Of the American poets the two who are easily masters of this form are Lowell and Mr. Aldrich, the former having a bold vigor of his own and the latter preferring rather an ingenious delicacy.

(1903). 129

VII

A NOTE ON THE QUATRAIN

ONE of the most stimulating contributions which M. Brunetière has made to criticism is his suggestion that each of the several kinds of poetry responds to a different demand of the human soul; and that therefore —since these demands are eternal—whenever we find any special kind of poetry apparently absent from any particular period in any literature, we are likely then to find it in illegitimate combination with one of the other kinds. If, for example, the pure lyric is not visible in French literature at a given moment, we may discover that either the dramatic or the epic poetry of France just then happens to be unduly lyric. If, to take another example, we perceive that the drama is not flourishing in English literature during a certain epoch,

A NOTE ON THE QUATRAIN

we are warranted in searching for an ex-
pansion of the dramatic element in the
epic of that epoch—the epic being held
to include its prose brother, the novel.

There were nine Muses in Greece of old,
and to every one is committed the guardian-
ship of a single art; and if any of them
may chance to be faint and weary, one of
her sisters is ever ready to take up her
burden and to bear it for her until her
strength returns. The arts came into being
to satisfy the needs of man; and the needs
of man vary only a little with the lapse of
the years. Every one who has ever had
occasion to compare the literatures of the
ancients with the literatures of the moderns,
must gladly have noted now and again the
serene and Attic simplicity of some latter-
day achievements and must have remarked
once more the eternal and surprising freshness of some masterpiece of antiquity.

One of the precious treasures which we
have happily inherited from the past is the
collection which is known as the 'Greek

Anthology,' and which contained the lesser, rather than the larger, of the lyrical effusions of that race of poets who were ever seeking the utmost perfection of phrase and the utmost purity of emotion. They recall to us not the mighty art of the Parthenon frieze, but rather the graceful and delicate workmanship of the Tanagra figurines. They may sometimes stretch themselves to the length of the idyl, but more often they are content to shrink to the modest dimensions of the epigram. And the epigram of the Greeks was not like ours; it was not a neatly turned witticism with a snap of the whip at the end of it; it was rather a single, simple thought, compressed into a few lines, ingenious in expression, and exquisite in sentiment. As Lord Neaves says, the "true or the best form of the early Greek epigram does not aim at wit or seek to produce surprise; its purpose is to set forth in the shortest, simplest, plainest language, but yet with perfect purity and even elegance of diction, some fact or

feeling of such interest as would prompt
the real or supposed speaker to record it."

More than one eulogist of the 'Greek
Anthology' has bepraised it as a manifes-
tation of the Greek genius without any
equivalent in modern literature. In its
own special field it may be without any
equal in our latter-day poetry; but in so
far as we are men like the Greeks with
emotions akin to theirs, it is not likely to
be wholly without any equivalent. Even
though no modern collection exists properly to be compared with the 'Greek Anthology,' the elements of such a collection
must be scattered here and there awaiting
the pious offices of a devoted collector.
In no modern literature is there a lack of
brief lyrics, wherein the singers of our own
time have voiced their sentiments, simply
and effectively. Although our modern epigram is not the epigram of the Greeks, none
the less has the Greek epigram its analogues
in our literature, even if we do not know
them by the Greek name. The 'Days' of

Emerson, for example, and his 'Letters,' and his 'Forbearance' are worthy of the 'Greek Anthology' so far as their simple elevation is concerned and the felicity of their phrasing.

It is true that the Athenian specimens of star-dust are unrhymed; and that ever since the Middle Ages we have more often than not preferred to rhyme our lyrics. Ever since the Renascence, indeed, we have revealed a tendency not only to rhyme, but to arrange our rhymes according to a pattern. It is in the sonnet that the poets of the past four centuries have been wont to express those uncomplicated feelings for which the Greeks held their own epigram to be sufficient. The Greek had found his advantage in adopting a rather rigid metrical scheme for his lesser lyric; and we moderns have felt a like aid in the strict structure of the sonnet. A lyrist is at once restrained and sustained by a fixed form, the framework of rhyme making the task easier than it seemed, since the necessary words may often spur the lagging fancy. On the other hand, the limitations of the rhyming scheme, though they may help the weakling, make even more difficult the achievement of the highest perfection.

The modern sonnet has thus an obvious analogy to the brief lyric of the 'Greek Anthology;' and it seems as though it might have also occasionally a certain relation to the Greek ode—or at least to some single member of that ode. Perhaps it may be a little fanciful to suggest that if Milton had been a Greek, born before the sonnet had been devised and before rhyme had been elaborated, he might have utilized in an ode the righteous wrath which inspired the noble and sonorous sonnet on the 'Late Massacre in Piedmont'—"Avenge, O Lord, Thy slaughtered saints." And of a certainty it would have been possible for Lowell to use the sonnet-form for his imaginative interpretations of Washington and of Lincoln.

There is, however, another modern form

which would demand abundant representation in any attempt to prepare a latter-day
equivalent to the 'Greek Anthology.' This
is the quatrain, which many a modern
lyrist, more especially in English, has
chosen as the form in which to express a
thought or a sentiment not rich enough for
the comparative amplitude of the sonnet.
Just as the sonnet has established itself
solidly in English poetry, while the other
fixed forms, the ballade and the rondeau
and their lesser brethren, are scarcely yet
acclimated amongst us, so the quatrain has
been accepted, while the *sixain,* the *huitain*
and the *dixain*—to give the French titles
to these poems of a single stanza of six,
and eight, and ten lines—have tempted
only a very few of those who write English.
If one of our poets cannot say what he
wants to say in four lines, he is likely to
say it in fourteen. If what he has to say
is not important enough for the ambitious
fourteener, he is likely to strive to condense
it into the single stanza of four lines.

A NOTE ON THE QUATRAIN

The sonnet has been discussed and ana-
lyzed and belauded; but the quatrain has
never received its due recognition. It has
made its way without loud heralding—such
as accompanied the revival of the ballade,
for instance. It has won its wide popularity
modestly and by dint of merit alone. Poets
have made use of it apparently without
thinking of it as a fixed form—if, indeed,
it can fairly be so entitled. In fact, the
sole poet who seems to have proclaimed
its worth is Mr. Frank Dempster Sherman,
who used the form itself to sing its own
praise:

> Hark at the lips of this pink whorl of shell
>   And you shall hear the ocean's surge and roar;
> So in the quatrain's measure, written well,
>   A thousand lines shall all be sung in four!

As the Greek epigram served for votive
tables so the quatrain has been chosen by
several American poets for memorial inscriptions wherein a lapidary concision was
needful. For the beautiful windows put
up in St. Margaret's, Westminster, in mem-

ory of Raleigh and of Milton, the inscriptions were written by Lowell and Whittier. Here is Lowell's quatrain on Raleigh:

The New World's Sons, from England's breast we
    drew
Such milk as bids remember whence we came;
Proud of her Past from which our Present grew,
    This window we erect to Raleigh's name.

And here is Whittier's on Milton:

The New World honors him whose lofty plea
For England's freedom made her own more sure,
Whose song, immortal as its theme, shall be
    Their common freehold while both worlds endure.

Whittier wrote another quatrain for the memorial tablet to Mrs. Sigourney, in Christ Church, Hartford:

She sang alone, ere womanhood had known
    The gift of song which fills the air today:
Tender and sweet, a music all her own
    May fitly linger where she knelt to pray.

And Lowell has preserved in the latest volume of his poems the inscription he had prepared for a soldiers' and sailors' monument in Boston:

138

A NOTE ON THE QUATRAIN

To those who died for her on land and sea,
That she might have a country great and free,
Boston builds this: build ye her monument
In lives like theirs, at duty's summons spent.

This has not a little of the stately elevation we admire in the best inscriptions of
the 'Greek Anthology.' But Lowell used
the quatrain not only to honor the dead
but also to carry a greeting of affection to
the living. On the seventy-fifth birthday
of Asa Gray, the foremost of American
botanists received congratulations from all
parts of the country; and among them were
these four lines from Lowell:

Just fate, prolong his file, well spent,
Whose indefatigable hours
Have been as gayly innocent
And fragrant as his flowers.

Lowell, indeed, not only sent a quatrain
as an appropriate salutation, but he also
received one on his own birthday from a
younger poet, Mr. Richard Watson Gilder:

Navies nor armies can exalt the state,—
Millions of men, nor coined wealth untold:
Down to the pit may sink a land of gold;
But one great name can make a country great.

The same lyrist has chosen the quatrain also to contain his praise of the 'Washington Monument, at Washington, D. C.':

Straight soars to heaven the white magnificence,—
    Free as man's thought, high as one lonely name.
True image of his soul,—serene, immense,—
    Mightiest of monuments and mightiest fame.

It was to a still younger American poet, H. C. Bunner—whose life was cut short almost in his youth—that we owe another 'To a Hyacinth Plucked for Decoration Day,' which has not a little of the Attic fragrance and felicity:

O Flower, plucked before the dew
Could wet thy thirsty petals blue—
Grieve not! a dearer dew for thee
Shall be the tears of memory.

Another of Bunner's quatrains deals also with death; this is the vigorous address 'To a Dead Woman':

Not a kiss in life; but one kiss, at life's end,
    I have set on the face of Death in trust for thee.
Through long years keep it fresh on thy lips, O
    friend!
    At the gate of Silence give it back to me.

A NOTE ON THE QUATRAIN

To many careless readers Bunner's name is known only as that of a humorist; but he had also the sentiment and the pathos which are ever characteristics of the true humorist, who is more than a manufacturer of inexpensive jests. An earlier writer of light verse, George Arnold, had also his more serious side, which never found deeper expression than in his quatrain called 'An Autobiography':

I was born some time ago, but I know not why:
  I have lived,—I hardly know either how or where:
Some time or another, I suppose, I shall die;
  But where, how or when, I neither know nor care!

Here, after this vain vaunting, it may be well to place another of Lowell's quatrains, one of the little group which he entitled 'Sayings':

In life's small things be resolute and great
To keep thy muscles trained; know'st thou when Fate
Thy measure takes, or when she'll say to thee,
"I find thee worthy; do this deed for me?"

To places opportunity may come, as well

as to persons, as Mr. M. A. De Wolfe
Howe has suggested in his 'Distinction':

The village sleeps, a name unknown, till men
  With life-blood stain its soil, and pay the due
That lifts it to eternal fame,—for then
  'Tis grown a Gettysburg or Waterloo.

With this may be linked another suggestive quatrain, by Mr. Selden L. Whit-
comb, on 'Pain':

It changed the soul of one to sour
  And passionate regret;
To one it gave unselfish power
  To love and to forget.

It was to one of the undergraduate pub-
lications of Columbia University that this
was contributed; and from the same
monthly may be taken two other quatrains, dealing each of them with one of
these names which it is well for the young
to learn to love. The first is by Mr. Walter
G. Kellogg:

If the gods would grant some favor to my Muse,
  And let me sound a sweet yet potent note,
This boon above all others would I choose,
  That I might write as dear old Herrick wrote.

And the second is from the pen of a scholar-poet, still connected with Columbia, Mr. Joel E. Spingarn. It has for its theme the English lyrist, who perhaps appeals most ardently to all youthful lovers of poetry—Keats:

> The Star of Fame shines down upon the river,
>   And answering the Stream of Life repeats:
> "Upon our waters shall be writ forever
>   The name of Keats."

In a collection of 'Yale Verse' may be found a suggestive quatrain by Mr. Walter D. Makepeace, on a subject that has tempted not a few poets, 'Sleep':

> Down through the mist of half-forgotten things
>   Tired spirits sink beneath night's slumberous sea,
> And, lapped in dream-waves, hear soft murmurings
>   Of Life's blest prelude to Eternity.

No American poet has shown a more frequent preference for the quatrain than Mr. Thomas Bailey Aldrich, and no one has better understood at once its possibilities and its limitations. He has unerring certainty of touch; and he never makes the mistake of distending into a sonnet a thought that would be better compacted into a quatrain. Consider, for example, how graceful and how charming are the four lines which he has called 'Memories':

Two things there are with Memory will abide,
　Whatever else befall, while life flows by:
That soft cold hand-touch at the altar side;
　The thrill that shook you at your child's first cry.

And contrast that quatrain with this, which he has aptly entitled 'Pessimist and Optimist':

This one sits shivering in Fortune's smile,
　Taking his joy with bated, doubtful breath:
This other, gnawed by hunger, all the while
　Laughs in the teeth of Death.

Other American poets there are who have delighted in the quatrain; and three further quotations may be adduced to bring out even more clearly the advantage of the condensed form. One is by Mr. Walter Learned, and he calls it 'Burning the Love-Letters':

Ashes to ashes, dust to dust,
　When life has quit the mortal frame.
When Love is at his last, we must
　Bury him thus, with flame to flame.

The second is by Mr. Edwin Markham, who has taken for his theme, 'Poetry':

She comes like the hush and beauty of the night,
  And sees too deep for laughter;
Her touch is a vibration and a light
  From worlds before and after.

And the third is due to Mr. William H. Hayne, who was moved to melody by musing 'On a Bust of Mendelssohn':

His high-arched brow and quiet eyelids seem
Brushed by the wings of some celestial dream—
A bird of passage whose melodious breath
Dispersed in music the wan mist of Death.

In this attempt to draw attention to the quatrain as a definite form, excellently devised for the expression of a lyric emotion not ample enough for the more spacious sonnet, the illustrations here selected have all been taken from our own American poets, partly because the quatrain has been cherished rather more by our native lyrists than by their British contemporaries, and also partly because the thoughts they have to express are a little more likely to appeal to us than are the sentiments voiced by our kin across the sea, who are at once so like us and so unlike us. Certain of the Victorian poets have abundantly employed the stern simplicity of the quatrain—Mr. William Watson, for one; and omission must not be made of the fact that in St. Margaret's, Westminster, besides the two windows adorned with the commemorative quatrains of Lowell and of Whittier, are two others bearing inscriptions also in four lines each by Tennyson and Browning.

(1903).

VIII

CAROLS OF COOKERY

IN one of the preliminary epistles contained in the opening pages of a poem on the 'Art of Cookery,' published in London in 1709, the author presents historic instances to support the lofty eminence upon which he establishes the art he is going immediately to eulogize in several hundred heroic couplets. "Indeed, Cookery," so he declares solemnly, "has an Influence upon Men's Actions even in the highest Stations of human Life. The great Philosopher Pythagoras, in his 'Golden Verses,' shews himself to be extremely nice in Eating, when he makes it one of his chief Principles of Morality to abstain from *Beans*. The noblest Foundations of Honour, Justice and Integrity were found to lye hid in Turnips, as appears in that great *Dictator, Cincinnatus,* who went from the Plough to the Command of the *Roman Army;* and having brought home Victory, retir'd to his Cottage: For when the Samnite Ambassadors came thither to him, with a large Bribe, and found him dressing *Turnips* for his Repast, they immediately return'd with this Sentence, 'That it was impossible to prevail upon him that could be contented with such a Supper.' In short, there are no honorary Appellations but what may be made use of to *Cooks;* for I find throughout the whole Reign of *Charlemain,* that the *Great Cook* of the *Palace* was one of the prime Ministers of State, and Conductor of Armies."

This metrical 'Art of Cookery' is avowedly modelled upon the 'Art of Poetry' of Horace. This bard of the buttery, this lyrist of the larder, this songster of the serving-room, tells us that

A Prince who in a Forest rides astray,
And weary to some Cottage finds the way,
Talks of no Pyramids of Fowl or Bisks of Fish,

CAROLS OF COOKERY

But hungry sups his Cream serv'd up in Earthen
  Dish:
Quenches his Thirst with Ale in nut-brown Bowls,
And takes the hasty Rasher from the Coals:
Pleas'd as King *Henry* with the Miller free,
Who thought himself as good a Man as He.

The poet is abundant in advice, and he bids

You that from pliant Paste wou'd Fabricks raise,
Expecting thence to gain immortal Praise,
Your Knuckles try, and let your Sinews know
Their Power to knead, and give the Form to Dough,
Chuse your Materials right, your seas'ning fix,
And with your Fruit resplendent Sugar mix;
From thence of course the Figure will arise,
And Elegance adorn the Surface of your Pies.

He is apt in axiom, and he declares that

If you wou'd have me merry with your Cheer
Be so yourself, or so at least appear.

And he asks pertinently:

Unless some Sweetness at the Bottom lye,
Who cares for all the crinkling of the Pye?

But even in pastry he is against undue extravagance:

Next let Discretion moderate your Cost,
And when you treat, three Courses be the most.

149

Let never fresh Machines your Pastry try,
Unless Grandees or Magistrates are by,
Then you may put a Dwarf into a Pye.
Or if you'd fright an Alderman and Mayor,
Within a Pasty lodge a living Hare;
Then midst their gravest Furs shall Mirth arise,
And all the Guild pursue with joyful Cries.

Perhaps the most characteristic passage in the whole poem is that wherein Horace himself is invoked, and wherein the likeness of the poet to the pastry-cook is formally established:

Were *Horace,* that great Master, now alive,
A Feast with Wit and Judgment he'd contrive.
As thus—supposing that you wou'd rehearse
A labour'd Work, and every Dish a Verse.
He'd say, mend this, and t'other Line, and this;
If after Tryal it were still amiss,
He'd bid you give it a new Turn of Face,
Or set some Dish more curious in its Place,
If you persist he wou'd not strive to move
A Passion so delightful as Self-love.

We shou'd submit our Treats to Criticks View,
And ev'ry prudent Cook shou'd read *Bossu.*
Judgment provides the Meat in Season fit,
Which by the Genius drest, its Sauce is wit.
Good Beef for Men, Pudding for Youth and Age,
Come up to the Decorum of the Stage.

CAROLS OF COOKERY

The Critick strikes out all that is not just,
And 'tis ev'n so the Butler chips his Crust.
Poets and Pastry-Cooks will be the same,
Since both of them their Images must frame.
Chimera's form the Poet's Fancy show,
The Cook contrives his Shapes in real Dough.

Thus wrote a British imitator of the
Roman songster of society in the early
part of the eighteenth century; and in the
later part of the nineteenth century an
American imitator of Horace, the late
Eugene Field, seems to have been moved
by a like impulse. Without going so far
as to identify poet and pastry-cook, he
felt called upon to hymn the praise of
'Rare Roast Beef,' and of 'Gosling Stew'
and of 'Apple Pie and Cheese.' Of these
three lilting lyrics, each with a culinary
ecstasy of its own, the third is by far the
best worth quoting here. It has the flavor
of New England, beyond all question; it
is not without a gusto of its own; and the
writer evidently revelled in his adroit alter-
nation of double and single rhymes;—
'Apple Pie and Cheese':

RECREATIONS OF AN ANTHOLOGIST

Full many a sinful notion
  Conceived of foreign powers
Has come across the ocean
  To harm this land of ours;
And heresies called fashions
  Have modesty effaced,
And baleful, morbid passions
  Corrupt our native taste.
O tempora! O mores!
  What profanations these
That seek to dim the glories
  Of apple pie and cheese!

 *   *   *   *   *   *

De gustibus, 'tis stated,
  Non disputandum est.
Which meaneth, when translated,
  That all is for the best.
So let the foolish choose 'em
  The vapid sweets of sin,
I will not disabuse 'em
  Of the heresy they're in;
But I, when I undress me
  Each night, upon my knees
Will ask the Lord to bless me
  With apple pie and cheese!

It must be admitted, however, that the
British imitator of Horace and the American are not the only poets who have spoken
highly of the doubtful dish which the one

spells *Pye* and the other *pie*. Emerson, a loftier man than either of the others, beyond all question, penned no ode to pastry, it is true; what he had to say in its praise was said in prose, no doubt, and yet what more magnificent eulogy could he have bestowed than his simple query, addressed to those who sat at table with him and who had rejected his proffer of a wedge of pie, "But what is pie for?"

And Dr. Holmes, quoting this anecdote, asks permission to declare "that pie, often foolishly abused, is a good creature, at the right time and in angles of thirty or forty degrees," although "in semicircles and quadrants it may sometimes prove too much for delicate stomachs."

One of the writers who contributed to the 'Liber Scriptorum,' the Book of the Authors Club of New York, has therein ventured an explanation of the strange anomaly to which Dr. Holmes draws attention, that Emerson, an abandoned pie-eater as he was, never complained of dyspepsia, whereas Carlyle, although he was fed on the wholesome oatmeal of his native land, was forever at war with his stomach and "lived with half his self-consciousness habitually centred beneath his diaphragm." The explanation proffered by the member of the Authors Club is as simple as it is alluring; there was so total and complete a sympathy between the American sage and the Scotch humorist that for the first time in recorded history we can behold the phenomenon of the Transfusion of Indigestion. In other words, Emerson ate the pie and Carlyle had the dyspepsia!

Of all the pies that are prevalent throughout the great American Pie-Belt, it may be admitted at once that the mince is, perhaps, the most deadly, but it cannot be denied that the pumpkin is the most characteristically American, if not also the most popular. Twice have simple lyrists lifted up their voices to carol forth the proper praise of this delightful dish. The first of these is anonymous; and it was in 1818 that he contributed to the Boston *Sentinel* these stanzas inspired by sincere enthusiasm, the 'Pumpkin Pye.'

The bards of the Hudson may sing of the melon,
  Its smooth, jetty seeds and its ripe, ruddy core,
And the feast of the reaper with ecstasy dwell on,
  Reclining at noon on the cool, breezy shore;
For me, the rich soil of New England produces
  An offering more dear to the taste and the eye,
The bright yellow pumpkin—how mellow its juices,
  When temper'd with ginger, and bak'd into pye.

*   *   *   *   *   *   *

Then hail to the Muse of the pumpkin and onion!
  The Frenchman may laugh and the Englishman
    sneer
At the land of the Bible, and psalm book, and
    Bunyan,
  Still, still to my bosom her green hills are dear;
Her daughters are pure as her bright crystal
    fountains,
  And Hymen, if ever thy blessings I try,
O! give me the girl of my own native mountains,
  Who knows how to temper the sweet pumpkin pye.

The second was no less a poet than John Greenleaf Whittier, the laureate of New England, the singer who has given voice to the homely sentiments of his section more satisfactorily than any other. Perhaps it may be objected that he deals with the fruit wherefrom the pie is compounded than with the pie itself; but this objection is too trivial for discussion. Here is a stanza of Whittier's autumnal dithyramb on the pumpkin:

Ah! on Thanksgiving Day, when from East and from West,
From North and from South come the pilgrim and guest;
When the grey-haired New Englander sees round his board
The old broken links of affection restored;
When the care-wearied man seeks his mother once more,
And the worn matron smiles where the girl smiled before;
What moistens the lip and what brightens the eye,
What calls back the past like the rich pumpkin pie?

An earlier American poet than either of these has sung of an American dish more primitive than apple pie or pumpkin. When Joel Barlow—the maker of that great gun of poesy, the 'Columbiad,' now spiked in silence and rusting in oblivion—was at

Chambéry in Savoy in January, 1793, his thoughts turned homeward to his native land and to the toothsome simplicity of homely hasty-pudding. He was moved to prepare three cantos in commendation of

The sweets of Hasty-Pudding. Come, dear bowl,
Glide o'er my palate, and inspire my soul,
The milk beside thee, smoking from the kine,
Its substance mingle, married in with thine,
Shall cool and temper thy superior heat,
And save the pains of blowing while I eat.

A little later the poet's strain rises with the occasion, and he seeks to ascertain the lofty origin of the grateful dish he was decking with chaplets of couplets gathered in his distant exile:

Assist me first with pious toil to trace
Through wrecks of time, thy lineage and thy race;
Declare what lovely squaw, in days of yore,
(Ere great Columbus sought thy native shore)
First gave thee to the world; her works of fame
Have lived indeed, but lived without a name.
Some tawny Ceres, goddess of her days,
First learned with stones to crack the well-dried
    maize,
Through the rough sieve to shake the golden shower,
In boiling water stir the yellow flour;

The yellow flour, bestrewed and stirred with haste,
Swells in the flood and thickens to a paste,
Then puffs and wallops, rises to the brim,
Drinks the dry knobs that on the surface swim,
The knobs at last the busy ladle breaks,
And the whole mass her true consistence takes.

Even over in Europe, on the confines of France and Italy, he found the Indian corn transplanted and doing its duty nobly though in a foreign clime:

But man, more fickle, the bold license claims,
In different realms to give thee different names.
Thee the soft nations round the warm Levant
Polenta call, the French, of course, *Polente.*
E'en in thy native regions, now I blush
To hear the Pennsylvanians call thee *Mush!*
On Hudson's banks, while men of Belgic spawn
Insult and eat thee by the name *Suppawn.*
All spurious appellations, void of truth;
I've better known thee from my earliest youth—
Thy name is *Hasty-Pudding!* thus my sire
Was wont to greet thee fuming from his fire.

A curious comparison next invites us to set beside this epic praise of one of the ways of serving the products of our national plant, the maize, with a lighter lyric, wherein a negro balladist has sung the joys

158

that accompany another form, in which
Indian-meal may be prepared for the tempting of our palates. Here are two stanzas
of Mr. Paul Laurence Dunbar's poem,
'When the Co'n-Pone's Hot':

> Dey is times in life when Nature
>   Seems to slip a cog an' go,
> Jes' a-rattlin' down creation,
>   Lak an ocean's overflow;
> When the worl' jes' stahts a-spinnin'
>   Lak a pickaninny's top,
> An' yo' cup o' joy is brimmin'
>   Twell it seems about to slop.
> An' you feel jes' lak a racah
>   Dat is trainin' fu' to trot—
> When yo' mammy ses de blessin'
>   An' de co'n-pone's hot.

* * * * * *

> I have heerd o' lots o' sermons,
>   An' I've heerd o' lots o' prayers,
> An' I've listened to some singin'
>   Dat has tuk me up de stairs
> Of de Glory-Lan' an' set me
>   Jes' below de Mahster's th'one,
> An' have lef' my hawt singin'
>   In a happy aftahtone,
> But dem wu'ds so sweetly murmured
>   Seems to tech de softes' spot,
> When my mammy ses de blessin'
>   An' de co'n-pone's hot.

Hasty-pudding and corn-pone, nourishing as they are and estimable in every way, lack distinction a little; they smack of the log cabin and of the negro quarters; they would not appeal to the Little Brothers of the Rich. For them rather does the miserable goose fatten his unhealthy liver; for them the canvasback seeks out the wild celery; for them the terrapin fulfils the end of his existence. Mr. Herman Oelrichs has rhymed for us his regret that the Roman epicures had to depart this life without having tasted the terrapin; and it is evident that the sympathetic poet believes their lives to have been wasted, and worse than wasted, since they failed of the bliss they were most capable of appreciating.

And if terrapin would be a dish worthy of Horace, what would Thackeray have thought of it?' Thackeray penned the 'Ballad of Bouillabaisse,' and lent to that unsavoury and unsatisfactory mess—there is no other word for it than that!—the incomparable aroma of his playful pathos:

CAROLS OF COOKERY

This Bouillabaisse a noble dish is—
  A sort of soup or broth, or brew,
Or hotpotch of all sorts of fishes,
  That Greenwich never could outdo;
Green herbs, red peppers, mussels, saffron,
  Soles, onions, garlic, roach and dace;
All these you eat at Terré's tavern,
  In that one dish of Bouillabaisse.

Indeed, a rich and savory stew 'tis;
  And true philosophers, methinks,
Who love all sorts of natural beauties,
  Should love good victuals and good drinks.
And Cordelier or Benedictine
  Might gladly, sure, his lot embrace,
Nor find a fast-day too afflicting,
  Which served him up a Bouillabaisse.

The sentimental visitors to Marseilles who seek out a proper place to try to like that untempting dish, are rarely honest enough with themselves to admit that it is not the dish itself they have enjoyed, but the tenderness of Thackeray's touching verses:

Where are you, old companions trusty
  Of early days here met to dine?
Come, waiter! quick, a flagon crusty—
  I'll pledge them in the good old wine.

The kind old voices and old faces
My memory can quick retrace;
Around the board they take their places,
And share the wine and Bouillabaisse.

The learned Dr. Gross is a professor
in the University of Freiburg, and he is
the author of a most interesting and most
instructive treatise on the 'Beginnings of
Art,' in the pages of which he discusses
not only sculpture and architecture and
painting, but also music and the dance,
the drama and poetry. And some of the
readers of this paper who may have supposed that it was only in a sophisticated
period of high development and of abundant leisure that man could spare time to
rhyme recipes and to chant the charm of
cookery, will be surprised to learn that this
was a habit also of primitive man. "The
lyric poetry of hunting tribes," so Dr.
Gross assures us, "very rarely soars to a
higher flight; it rather abides with unmis-
takable preference in the lower regions of
sensuality. The coarsest material pleas-

ures occupy a very large space in primitive verse; and we do these poets no wrong when we say that their lyric inspiration is quite as often of the stomach as of the heart. It must indeed appear a real sacrilege to an ideal æsthete that we presume to pass off the eating and drinking songs of the Australians and Botocudos, especially as poetical productions. They are, nevertheless, such, as they are truly expressions of feeling in verbal rhythmic form. No feeling is in and of itself poetic; and there is no feeling which cannot be made poetical if it is expressed in an æsthetic form for an æsthetic purpose. It may, moreover, soften the indignation that arises against the use that is made here of the name of poetry, if we recollect that even the tenderest lyric poets of civilization occasionally do not consider it unworthy of them to extol the pleasures of the table."
(1900).

IX

RECIPES IN RHYME

"**B**OOKS**," said that acute critic, Walter Bagehot, "are for various purposes: tracts, to teach; almanacs, to sell; poetry, to make pastry." The British scoffer did not foresee that a Gallic dramatist, the author of 'Cyrano de Bergerac,' would one day set upon the stage a pastry cook who should be also a poet and who would be therefore able to declare the eternal principles of the culinary art in imperishable rhyme. It is this Ragueneau of M. de Rostand who thus sets forth the proper manner of preparing that delectable dish known as 'Les Tartelettes Amandines':

> Battez, pour qu'ils soient mousseux
> Quelques œufs;
> Incorporez à leur mousse
> Un jus de cédrat choisi;
> Versez-y
> Un bon lait d'amande douce;

Mettez de la pâte à flan
    Dans le flanc
De moules à tartelette;
D'un doigt preste, abricotez
    Les côtés;
Versez goutte à gouttelette

Votre mousse en ces puits, puis
    Que ces puits   `
Passant au four, et, blondines,
Sortant en gais troupelets,
    Ce sont les
Tartelettes amandines!

And this has been rendered readily into
English rhymes by Gertrude Hall, thus:
'Almond Cheese Cakes':

Briskly beat to lightness due,
    Eggs a few;
With the eggs so beaten, beat—
Nicely strained for this same use—
    Lemon juice,
Adding milk of almonds, sweet.

With fine pastry dough, rolled flat,
    After that,
Line each little scalloped mould;
Round the sides, light-fingered, spread
    Marmalade;
Pour the liquid eggy gold,

Into each delicious pit;
Prison it
In the oven,—and, by and by,
Almond cheese cakes will in gay
Blonde array
Bless your nostril and your eye!

Another French dramatist, the younger Alexander Dumas, has caused a charming young lady in his comedy of 'Francillon' to declare the true formula of a Japanese salad—avowedly of her own invention. But this formula is in bald prose—nay, more, it is in the broken dialogue of the stage; and therefore it is inadmissible amid these recipes, more metrical, if not more musical. The so-called Japanese salad of the Frenchman is just a little too complicated to win favor in the eyes of American epicures, whose taste is simpler, less sophisticated—in a word, purer. In a salad the full flavor of the chief ingredient should be evoked directly by the dressing, the sharpness of the vinegar and the blandness of the oil uniting for the purpose. And this is why the British salads often lack a welcome from Americans; they are too fussy; they are not content to let well enough alone. It is this which vitiates the best known of all rhyming recipes—that of Sydney Smith, for a winter salad:

Two large potatoes passed through the kitchen sieve
Unwonted softness to the salad give.
Of mordant mustard add a single spoon—
Distrust the condiment which bites too soon.
But deem it not, thou man of herbs, a fault
To add a double quantity of salt.
Three times the spoon with oil of Lucca crown,
And once with vinegar procured from town.
True flavor needs it, and your poet begs
The pounded yellow of the two well-boiled eggs.
Let onion atoms lurk within the bowl,
And unsuspected animate the whole.
And, lastly, on the flavored compound toss
A magic teaspoon of anchovy sauce.
Then though green turtle fail, though venison's
    tough,
And ham and turkey are not boiled enough,
Serenely full the epicure may say,
"Fate cannot harm me—I have dined to-day!"

The verse is brisk enough, whatever may be thought of the moral; and the reverend rhymester has set a model for a host of later poetasters (perhaps even one might here venture on an orthography more appropriate, however inaccurate, and style these imitators of the good dean—poet-tasters). The most of these followers of Sydney Smith are nameless; they have failed to tag themselves to their formulas, from modesty, perhaps, and perhaps from carelessness. Here, for example, are two sets of versified directions for compounding the delectable plum pudding. The first of them is of British authorship, apparently, and also of a stricter orthodoxy; a 'Poetical Recipe for English Plum Pudding':

To make a plum pudding to Englishmen's taste,
So all may be eaten and nothing be waste,
Take of raisins, and currants, and bread crumbs all
    round;
Also suet from oxen, and of flour a pound.
Of citron well candied, or lemon as good,
With molasses and sugar, eight ounces, I would.
Into this first compound next must be hasted
A nutmeg well grated, ground ginger well tasted,
Then of milk half a pint, and of fresh eggs take six;
Be sure after this that you properly mix.
Next tie up in a bag, just as round as you can,
Put it into a capacious and suitable pan,
Then boil for eight hours just as hard as you can.

The second seems rather to be of American origin, although in such matters exact accuracy is difficult of attainment and the poet without a name is likely to prove a man without a country unless his speech betrayeth him;—'Plum Pudding':

> Aunt Betsy makes good pudding,
>   And you can likewise do it
> If you follow her directions:
>   "Take half a pound of suet,
> Three quarter pounds of bread crumbs fine,
> Two tablespoons of brandy wine.
> One and a quarter pounds of fruit,
> A pinch of grated ginger root,
> Quarter-pound moist sugar—brown—
> A single nutmeg grated down,
> Two tablespoons of milk or cream
> (The latter is best, I deem)
> Four eggs—and just enough molasses
> To fill one of your small wine-glasses—
> Then steam five hours." I'm sure you'll say
> "No better cook than Betsy Leigh."

The model set by Sydney Smith has been followed also by Mr. Adolph Meyer in a string of couplets wherein he praises one of the foremost of American contributions to the resources of the gastronomic art. In spite of his Teutonic name, the poet is probably an American—although it is to be recalled always that the dish he celebrates has been accepted in France also, infrequent as have been French borrowings from the kitchens of other countries. Here are Mr. Meyer's verses—and it is chiefly in his final quatrain that he recalls the prescription of the earlier Englishman:—'Lobster à l'Américaine':

A lobster full of life you need,
But, ere you further shall proceed,
Drop him within a copper pot
That's filled with water boiling-hot.
When boiled, then him in eighths divide,
Now turn these oft from side to side
In butter simmering in a pan,
And do this careful as you can,
And salt and pepper ere you cease.
Of garlic crush a little piece,
This with a glass of Chablis add—
Your lobster then cannot be bad.
Skin six tomatoes and take out the seed;
Do this as thoroughly as it may need.
Now with the lobster altogether cook,
And that the mixture does not burn, oft look.

A little spice would add unto the savor;
Bay-leaf and thyme have not too strong a flavor.
And after thirty minutes on the fire
The lobster's cooked. In peace you can retire.
Invite your friends now to this treat
'Twould tempt a dying man to eat;
The sauce is better than the lobster, too.
Such dishes are, you will agree with me, too few,
This dainty feast would surely animate
The most despondent, melancholic pate;
He will give thanks when he in truth can say,
" 'Twas Lobster à l'Americaine to-day."

It is true that some iconoclast, ever swift to upset tradition, may be ready to prove that "lobster American style" is French, after all, and in spite of its name. But the nationality of another preparation of shellfish is indisputable; and the rollicking rhymester who has lyrically recorded the proper method to be employed in its concoction would stand revealed as an American, even though his name was wholly unknown. For where else do clams dwell except in America? They are citizens of the United States by nativity; and it was a worthy patriotism that inspired Mr. W.

A. Croffut to proclaim the transcendent and most appetizing flavor of 'Clam Soup':

First catch your clam—along the ebbing edges
Of saline coves you'll find the precious wedges,
With backs up, lurking in the sandy bottom;
Pull in your iron rake, and lo! you've got 'em.
Take thirty large ones, put a basin under,
And cleave with knife the stony jaws asunder;
Add water (three quarts) to the native liquor,
Bring to a boil (and, by the war, the quicker
It boils the better, if you'd do it cutely),
Now add the clams, chopped up and minced min-
    utely.
Allow a longer boil of just three minutes,
And while it bubbles quickly stir within its
Tumultuous depths, where still the mollusks mutter,
Four tablespoons of flour and four of butter,
A pint of milk, some pepper to your notion,
And clams need salting, although born of ocean.
Remove from fire (if much boiled they will suffer,
You'll find that India-rubber isn't tougher);
After 'tis off, add three fresh eggs well beaten,
Stir once more, and it's ready to be eaten.
Fruit of the wave! oh, dainty and delicious!
Food for the gods! ambrosia for Apicius!
Worthy to thrill the soul of sea-born Venus,
Or titillate the palate of Silenus.

It is not in the United States, but in Great Britain, that one must seek the songster of the swan. The cygnets of Norwich are eaten before the end of November, being cooked on a spit according to the directions thus rhythmically preserved:

Take three pounds of beef fat, beat in a mortar.
Put it into the swan, that is, when you've caught her;
Some pepper, salt, mace, some nutmeg, an onion,
Will heighten the flavor in gourmand's opinion.
Then tie up tight with a small piece of tape,
That the gravy and other things may not escape.
A meal paste, rather thick, should be laid on the
    breast,
And some whited brown paper should cover the rest.
Fifteen minutes at least ere the swan you take down;
Pull the paste off the bird that the breast may get
    brown.

The Gravy

To a gravy of beef, good and strong, I opine,
You'd be right if you add half a pint of port wine:
Pour this through the swan; yes, quite through the
    belly;
Then serve the whole up with some hot currant jelly.

Would not the opinion of Pythagoras concerning wild fowl have been modified perforce if he had ever tasted a young swan thus artfully prepared—or if he had ever had the good fortune to find before

173

him the even more toothsome canvasback duck, as yet unsung by any bard?

Hawthorne has told us of a dream he had once "that the world had become dissatisfied with the inaccurate manner in which facts are reported, and had employed him at a salary of a thousand dollars to relate things of importance exactly as they happen." Here is a valuable suggestion, fit for instant use. If any philanthropist is at a loss how to lay out his money to advantage, let him employ half a dozen or half a score of minor poets, deft in the adjustment of rhymes, and set them to singing the praises of the good things of life and to putting into immortal verse the best ways of cooking this or that delectable dish. Thus should the lyrist and the culinary artist collaborate for the benefit of posterity. Men of science tell us that rhymes and jingles linger in the ear longer than mere prose; and recipes likely to be lost if left in perishable prose might aspire to a lofty longevity if fixed in verse.

Here is a case in point. The sack-posset is now no longer concocted; and even the most learned compounder of American drinks would be puzzled if a sack-posset were suddenly demanded. Yet, though the thing itself be vanished from the face of the earth, the formula used in mixing it has survived in verse for now more than a century and a half. In February, 1744, in the *Gazette* of Bradford, the New York printer gave "a receipt for all young ladies that have an eye to matrimony,"—'To Make a Sack-Posset':

From famed Barbados, on the western main,
Fetch sugar half a pound; fetch sack from Spain
A pint; and from the East India coast
Nutmeg, the glory of our Northern toast;
O'er flaming coals together let them heat
Till the all-conquering sack dissolves the sweet;
O'er such another fire set eggs, twice ten,
New born, the product of the wedded hen;
Stir them with steady hand, and conscience pricking
To see the untimely fate of twenty chicken;
From shining shelf take down your brazen skillet,
A quart of milk from gentle cow will fill it;
When boiled and cooled, put milk and sack to egg,

Unite them firmly like the triple league;
Then, covered close, together let them dwell
Till miss twice sings, "You must not kiss and
  tell,"
Then, lad and lass, snatch up your eager spoon,
And fall on fiercely, like a starved dragoon.

Although this has been borrowed from one of the earliest of American newspapers, its authorship is probably British; indeed, one may doubt whether there was in all his Majesty's colonies in 1744 any one having command over light and easy versification of this sort. The technical skill of the Bacchanalian instructor may not be worthy of the very highest praise, yet, none the less, it is beyond the possession of any of the American versifiers of that early day,— even if they had deigned to bestow their attention upon the poetic aspects of the culinary art.

After the lapse of a century and a half, more than one lyrist has arisen in the United States ready to preserve in verse the proper method of preparing one or another of the American national dishes.

The doughnut, the descendant of the Dutch oilcake, that first cousin of the Knicker-bocker cruller:

> One cup of sugar, one cup of milk;
> Two eggs beaten fine as silk,
> Salt and nutmegs (lemon 'll do) ;
> Of baking-powder, teaspoons two.
> Lightly stir the flour in;
> Roll in pie-board not too thin;
> Cut in diamonds, twists, or rings.
> Drop with care the doughy things
> Into fat that briskly swells
> Evenly the spongy cells.
> Watch with care the time for turning;
> Fry them brown—just short of burning.
> Roll in sugar, serve when cool.
> Price—a quarter for this rule.

And even corn-pone has been embalmed in rhyme by a right reverend bard—the corn-pone which the white American rarely gets nowadays, although the red American rarely made it (or its equivalent) before the white American came across the Atlantic, and although the black American best appreciates the delicacy of its proper preparation. It was an American Bishop

RECREATIONS OF AN ANTHOLOGIST

(William of Connecticut) who followed
the ecclesiastical precedent of the English
dean, and proclaimed the only true way
of making the humble dish:

Take a cup of corn-meal, and the meal should be
   yellow;
Add a cup of wheat flour for to make the corn
   mellow;
Of sugar a cup, white or brown or your pleasure,
(The color is nothing, the fruit is the measure);

And now comes a troublesome thing to indite,
For the rhyme and the reason they trouble me quite;
For after the sugar, the flour, and the meal
Comes a cup of sour cream, but unless you should
   steal
From your neighbors, I fear you will never be able
This item to put upon your cook's table;
For "sure and indeed," in all town I remember,
Sour cream is as scarce as June buds in December.

So here an alternative nicely contrived
   Is suggested your mind to relieve,
And showing how you without stealing at all
   The ground that is lost may retrieve.
Instead of sour cream take one cup of milk,
   "Sweet milk!" what a sweet phrase to utter!
And to make it creamlike put into the cup
   Just three tablespoonfuls of butter.

RECIPES IN RHYME

Cream of tartar, one teaspoonful, rules dietic—
How nearly I wrote it down tartar emetic!—
But no; cream of tartar it is without doubt,
And so the alternative makes itself out.
Of soda the half of a teaspoonful add,
Or else your poor corn cake will go to the bad;
Two eggs must be broken without being beat,
Then of salt a teaspoonful your work will complete.
Twenty minutes of baking are needful to bring
To the point of perfection this "awful good thing."
To eat at the best this remarkable cake
You should fish all day long on the royal-named
    lake,
With the bright waters glancing in glorious light
And beauties outnumbered bewild'ring your sight,
On mountain and lake, in water and bay;
And then, when the shadows fall down from on high,
Seek "Sabbath Day Point," as the light fades away,
And end with this feast the angler's long day,
Then, there will you find, without any question,
That an appetite honest awaits on digestion.

British again are the three following,
clipped years ago from a newspaper and
derived originally, it may be, from the
collection of *Mr. Punch*. They are entitled
'Extracts from the Commonplace-Book of
a Connoisseur'; and the first is a recipe
for 'Pigeon Soup':

179

"Eight pigeons take, all pluck, and two, the worst,
Review, *i.e.*, cut up, and drown the pair
In water that will fill a large tureen.
Necks, gizzards, pinions, livers of the rest
Add, and boil well, and strain. Season the birds,
But part dissected, with your pungent spice,
Mixed spice and salt—English, you understand,
Not attic; that, perchance, you lack—and then
Truss them as if their little toes were cold,
Legs into belly. Pick and wash and shred
Parsley, young onions, spinach eke; and grate
Bread, say a handful. In the frying-pan
A lump of butter put, and when it boils,
Throw in your bread, and, mind you, do it brown.
Put on the stock to boil, and add the birds,
Herbs, and fried bread, and when the doves are done,
Of course they may be dished.
                        —'Massacre of the Innocents.'

The second considers 'Cocky Leeky':

Scrag of mutton, shank of veal,
From the butcher where you deal;
Good beef stock is even better—
Now, then, follow to the letter:
Portly fowl, with leeks, say three,
Pepper, salt, judiciously.
Leeks cut up in inch-long pieces;
Slowly boil. When it decreases,
After a good hour or more,
Add three sliced leeks as before.

One hour longer let it bubble,
It will pay you for your trouble.
If you've followed as you should,
You'll declare the stuff is good.
—'Macbeth' (improved).

And the third deals with 'Stewed Oysters':

Friend am I, and not foe, and yet men beard me,
And boil my beard in my own juice with gravy;
Strain off my beard, and put me in instead,
Thicken the mess with flour and ounce of butter,
Kill my ambrosial flavor with their ketchup
(White wine, anchovy, lemon, what you will).
Nutmeg, and salt and pepper, mace and cream;
Simmer and serve me up on toasted sippets.
They will not let me boil, but my blood boils
At thought of how, while they would paint the lily,
Pepsine and piquant coolness both must perish.
—'The Foreboding Native.'

And at the end of this crisscrossing of the northern ocean, with quotations first from British bards and then from American artists in metre, it is to New York that a return is necessary again to quote here the chaplet of couplets written by the American who in his day enjoyed the widest fame as

a gastronomist, the late Samuel Ward, once
a banker in New York and later a lobbyist
in Washington—and always a good liver
and a good fellow. He called them 'Verses
for the Kitchen':

> Always have lobster sauce with salmon,
> And put mint sauce your roasted lamb on.

> In dressing salad mind this law—
> With two hard yolks use one that's raw.

> Roast veal with rich stock gravy serve;
> And pickled mushrooms, too, observe.

> Roast pork, *sans* apple sauce, past doubt
> Is 'Hamlet' with the *Prince* left out.

> Your mutton chops with paper cover
> And make them amber brown all over.

> Broil lightly your beefsteak—to fry it
> Argues contempt of Christian diet.

> To roast spring chicken is to spoil 'em—
> Just split 'em down the back and broil 'em.

> It gives true epicures the vapors
> To see boiled mutton minus capers.

182

RECIPES IN RHYME

The cook deserves a hearty cuffing
Who serves roast fowls with tasteless stuffing.

Smelts require egg and biscuit powder—
Don't put fat pork in your clam chowder.

Egg sauce—few make it right, alas!
Is good with bluefish or with bass.

Nice oyster sauce gives zest to cod—
A fish, when fresh, to feast a god.

But one might rhyme for weeks this way,
And still have lots of things to say.

And so I'll close, for, reader mine,
This is about the hour I dine.

Whether these 'Verses for the Kitchen'
are fairly to be included under the title of
this paper may be a matter of dispute; but
not to be debated is the fact that they are
far better in manner and in matter than
most of the other gastronomic effusions here
collected. They have the calm ease of a
man who knew what he was talking about

and who thought his opinion on the subject worthy of condensation into couplets, as sharp as carving-knives should be.

> The things we eat by various juice controul,
> The Narrowness or Largeness of the soul.
> Onions will make ev'n Heirs or Widows weep,
> The tender Lettice brings on softer Sleep.
> Eat Beef or Pye-crust if you'd serious be;
> Your shell-fish raises *Venus* from the Sea;
> For Nature that inclines to Ill or Good,
> Still nourishes our Passions by our Food.

So wrote the author of the 'Art of Cookery,' in imitation of Horace's 'Art of Poetry,' a work which is ascribed to the ingenious Dr. King; which was printed in London in 1709 for Bernard Lintott, at the Cross Keys between the two *Temple* Gates in *Fleet Street;* and which was humbly inscribed to the Honourable Beef Steak Club.

With one more quotation from Dr. King's sapient pages—if, indeed, this 'Art of Cookery' be of his inditing—this culinary anthology may fitly close:

184

RECIPES IN RHYME

'Tis a sage Question, if the Art of Cooks
Is lodg'd by Nature, or attained by Books;
That Man will never frame a noble Treat
Whose whole Dependence lies on some Receipt.
Then by pure Nature ev'ry thing is spoil'd,
She knows no more than stew'd, bak'd, roast, and
    boil'd.
When Art and Nature join th' effect will be
Some nice Ragoust, or charming Fricasy. `
   (1900).

X

THE UNCOLLECTED POEMS OF H. C. BUNNER

THE late H. C. Bunner published two volumes of poetry, 'Airs from Arcady' and 'Rowen: Second-Crop Songs.' But only a small proportion of his verse, comic and serious, is contained in these two little books. He was always modest in discussing his own work, in prose or in verse, yet he was ambitious also; and when he came to choose out those of his writings which he was willing to reprint in book form, he held up a high standard for himself. When his first volume of short stories, 'In Partnership,' was ready for the printer he became dissatisfied with one of his stories, and withdrew it, writing in its stead the vigorous and pathetic tale called

'A Letter and a Paragraph.' There is
also a long serial story, contributed to a
weekly paper, which he refused always to
reprint as a book, although it was an ab-
sorbingly dramatic narrative. In selecting
from his own verse he was even more particular. Perhaps this was due to the fact
that he was widely known as the editor
of *Puck,* and that if he had reprinted all
of even the best of his humorous verse
he would have been accepted only as a
comic poet. He was unwilling to have
the graceful and imaginative lyrics which
give distinction to 'Airs from Arcady' and
'Rowen' swamped by an undue proportion
of his lighter verse. In neither of these
volumes did he include any of his more
broadly comic pieces—like this sonnet,
for example, in which the reader is left
in doubt as to what manner of vessel it
is the poet is addressing:—'To a Schooner'.

O Brave and Beautiful! the purling foam
  Curls clinging with caressing touch around
  Thy curves symmetrical. My heart doth bound

187

At sight of thee—'neath native heavens' dome,
Or far abroad, where venturous Teutons roam.
Moist thy smooth sides as swiftly, without sound,
Across the Bar thou passest, brimmed and crowned
With thy rich freight, dearer than musty tome
To student's heart; sweet as the honey-comb.
Not wondrous caverns underneath the ground,
Dark treasure-caves of subterranean gnome,
Yield fairer boon than in thee I have found—
Peace! O, my blissful spirit's cherished home,
In yon dark flood lies Care forever drowned!

A pleasant flavor of the classics lingers
about the lines in which the poet set down
his dissatisfaction with 'Atlantic City':

O City that is not a city, unworthy the prefix At-
    lantic,
Forlornest of watering-places, and thoroughly Phila-
    delphian!
In thy despite I sing, with a bitter and deep detesta-
    tion—
A detestation born of a direful and dinnerless even-
    ing,
Spent in thy precincts unhallowed—an evening I
    trust may recur not.
Never till then did I know what was meant by the
    word god-forsaken:
Thou its betokening hast taught me, being the
    chiefest example.

Thou art the scorned of the gods; thy sand from
their sandals is shaken;
Thee have they left in their wrath to thy uninter-
esting extensiveness,
Barren and bleak and big; a wild aggregation of
barracks,
Miscalled hotels, and of dovecotes denominate cot-
tages;
A confusion of ugly girls, of sand, and of health-
bearing breezes,
With one unending plank-walk for a true Philadelphia "attraction."
City ambitiously named, why, with inducements
delusive,
Is the un-Philadelphian stranger lured to thy desert
pretentious?
'Tis not alone that thy avenues, broad and unpaved
and unending,
Re-echo yet with the obsolete music of 'Pinafore,'
Whistled in various keys by the rather too numerous
negro;
'Tis not alone that Propriety—Propriety too Phila-
delphian—
Over thee stretches an ægis of wholly superfluous
virtue;
That thou art utterly good; hast no single vice to
redeem thee;
'Tis not alone that thou art provincial in all things,
and petty;
And that the dulness of death is gay, compared to
thy dulness—

RECREATIONS OF AN ANTHOLOGIST

'Tis not alone for these things that my curse is to
rest upon thee:
But for a sin that crowns thee with perfect and emi-
nent badness;
Sets thee alone in thy shame, the unworthiest town
on the sea-coast:
THIS: that thou dinest at Noon, and then in a man-
ner barbarian,
Soupless and wineless and coffeeless, untimely and
wholly indecent—
As is the custom, I learn, in Philadelphia proper.
I rose and I fled from thy Supper; I said: "I will get
me a Dinner!"
Vainly I wandered thy streets: thy eating-places un-
godly
Knew not the holiness of Dinner; in all that evening
I dined not;
But in a strange low lair, infested of native me-
chanics,
BOLTED a fried beef-steak for the physical need of my
stomach.
And for them that have fried that steak, in Aïdes'
lowest back-kitchen
May they eternally broil, by way of a warning to
others.
During my wanderings, I met, and hailed with de-
light one Italian,
A man with a name from 'Pasquale'—the chap sung
by Tagliapietra—
He knew what it was to dine; he comprehended my
yearnings;

But the spell was also on him; the somnolent spell
    Philadelphian;
And his hostelry would not be open till Saturday
    next; and I cursed him.
Now this is not *too* much to ask, God knows, that a
    mortal should want a
Pint of Bordeaux to his dinner, and a small cigar-
    ette for a climax:
But, these things being denied him, where then is
    your Civilization?
O Coney Island! of old I have reviled and blas-
    phemed thee,
For that thou dowsest thy glim at an hour that is un-
    metropolitan;
That thy frequenters' feet turn townwards ere strik-
    eth eleven,
When the returning cars are filled with young men
    and maidens,
Most of the maidens asleep on the young men's cin-
    dery shoulders—
Yea, but I spake as a fool, insensate, disgruntled,
    ungrateful:
Thee will I worship henceforth in appreciative hu-
    mility:
Luxurious and splendid and urban, glorious and gas-
    lit and gracious,
Gathering from every land thy gay and ephemeral
    tenantry,
From the Greek who hails thee: "Thalatta!" to the
    rustic who murmurs "My Golly!"
From the Bowery youth who requests his sweetheart
    to "look at them billers!"

To the Gaul whom thy laughing waves almost per-
    suade to immersion:
O Coney Island, thou art the weary citizen's
    heaven—
A heaven to dine, not die in, joyful and restful and
    clamful,
Better one hour of thee than an age of Atlantic
    City!

And the same flavor, more pronounced,
is discoverable also in the daring rhymes
on 'Classic Journalism':

> The beautiful garland of justice awaits
> The eminent poet and general, Socrates.
>   KROPHUTIKOS GRAPHIKOS.
>   5th Century B. C.

A great thing was journalism in Greece,
When that nation was foremost in war and in peace.
I was long on the staff of the Athens *Courier,*
And the style the boys ran the machine you shall
    hear.
The boss paper it was the South-Spartan *Tribune,*
Which was owned by a man of the name of Laocoon;
And had a grand building, where down the two sides
Ran two rows of extra-sized Caryatides.
'Twas a very fine sheet, with a half-page of locals,
Done up in neat style by J. Themistocles.
At the top of its columns, its letter-heads, bills,

It flaunted the name of its founder, Achilles.
'Twas so high-toned, the boys used to say its chief
    writer
Was nobody less than Olympian Jupiter.
The staff boasted ladies galore, Hermione
Ran the fashion column entirely alone.
Cybele did the Art notes; the critical flail
Was skilfullly wielded by Mrs. Omphale.
But the Bœotian *Herald* beat this a long sight,
By engaging on glorious terms Aphrodite.
And the *Herald* had Hero, who later demeaned her-
Self by receiving the visits of Leander.
The East-Acarnanian *Times* made its gains
By the aid and assistance of Aristophanes.
When the Greeks sent their troops against Troy's
    forces meagre,
The *Times* dispatched war-correspondent Meleager.
Then there was the Attican *World,* that shocked
    Greece,
By opening its columns to Trojan Æneas;
But its editor well knew his sheet how to carry on;
Had a competent musical critic in Arion;
And knowing public fancy a feuilleton tickles,
He secured for that duty the well known Pericles.
The proprietor, he was a fellow of means,
Senior partner of Apollo and Diogenes.
Ah, those were great times, but they're all long gone
    by,
Like the days when I used to be sweet on Clytie;
And Greek journalism has vanished beneath
The silent, oblivious waters of Lethe.

193

This had been suggested by the couplet quoted from Mr. W. A. Croffut, who was then contributing to the now departed *Daily Graphic*. Another copy of verses had its origin in the allegation that a certain songster of the Sierras had written a poem in which the name of the author of 'Faust' was made to rhyme with the unpoetic word *teeth*. The American humorist unhesitatingly mispronounced the names Molière and Goethe, and wrote these stanzas on 'Shake, Mulleary and Go-ethe.'

I.

I have a bookcase, which is what
Many much better men have not.
There are no books inside, for books,
I am afraid, might spoil its looks.
But I've three busts, all second-hand,
Upon the top. You understand
I could not put them underneath—
Shake, Mulleary and Go-ethe.

II.

Shake was a dramatist of note;
He lived by writing things to quote,
He long ago put on his shroud:

194

Some of his works are rather loud.
His bald-spot's dusty, I suppose.
I know there's dust upon his nose.
I'll have to give each nose a sheath—
Shake, Mulleary and Go-ethe.

III.

Mulleary's line was quite the same;
He has more hair; but far less fame.
I would not from that fame retrench—
But he is foreign, being French.
Yet high his haughty head he heaves,
The only one done up in leaves.
They're rather limited on wreath—
Shake, Mulleary and Go-ethe.

IV.

Go-ethe wrote in the German tongue:
He must have learned it very young.
His nose is quite a but for scoff,
Although an inch of it is off.
He did quite nicely for the Dutch;
But here he doesn't count for much.
They all are off their native heath—
Shake, Mulleary and Go-ethe.

V.

They sit there, on their chests, as bland
As if they were not second-hand.
I do not know of what they think,

Nor why they never frown or wink.
But why from smiling they refrain
I think I clearly can explain:
They none of them could show much teeth—
Shake, Mulleary and Go-ethe.

In the early days of *Puck* the young
poet chose to consider himself a dweller
in the coast of Bohemia; and yet in more
than one of his poems of this period he
seems to have anticipated the time when
he should remove from the seaport of
Prague. This feeling is reflected more
fully in the verses which he entitled 'Wed'
than in any other of his poems, excepting
only, it may be, that called the 'Deserter.'
Here is 'Wed':

For these white arms about my neck—
  For the dainty room, with its ordered grace—
For my snowy linen without a fleck—
  For the tender charm of this uplift face—

For the softened light and the homelike air—
  The low luxurious cannel fire—
The padded ease of my chosen chair—
  The devoted love that discounts desire—

I sometimes think, when Twelve is struck
  By the clock on the mantel, tinkling clear,
I would take—and thank the gods for the luck—
  One single hour with the Boys and the Beer.

Where the sawdust scent of a cheap saloon
  Is mingled with malt; where each man smokes,
Where they sing the street songs out of tune,
  Talk Art, and bandy ephemeral jokes.

By Jove, I do! And all the time
  I know not a man that is there to-night
But would barter his brains to be where I'm—
  And I'm well aware that the beggars are right.

And here is its fellow lyric, the 'Deserter':

Scene.—In Bohemia.

Glad? Don't I say so? Aren't your fingers numb
    where
  They've felt the home-returning wanderer's grip?
Sit down? I will.
          Put my umbrella somewhere
          Where it won't drip.

My book—that parcel—thanks! What is it? Mrs.
  Barbauld's—no, I mean, Plato's Nursery
    Rhymes—
Burton's Anat—oh, never mind it! This is
        Just like old times.

197

RECREATIONS OF AN ANTHOLOGIST

Thank you, I *will* take something. No, not whiskey.
   I've cut that—oh dear, yes, of course! from
   choice.
One lemonade!   Jove! I feel younger—frisky—
         One of the boys.

Give an account? Oh, I've been quite the rover
   These two years—yes, I've only just got home.
Set out in April. Roughish passage over.
         Went first to Rome.

I stayed in Paris longer than I meant to:
   (I had to break the trip there coming back
From Rome.) Bonn was the next place that I went
   to—
         Met you there, Jack.

You, with an ancient relative and a Murray—
   Relative's dead? I hope he . . . . ? Ah, that's
   right!
I say, what made you leave in such a hurry,
         On Christmas night?

I got engaged that last week in December.
   —Didn't you meet the Carletons in Bordeaux?
You knew the girls. Mine's Florry. You remem-
   ber—
         The blonde, you know.

You—what? God bless me! And you were refused,
   eh?

Of course you were. That's why you looked so
    blue
That Christmas? Ya-as! I called the following
    Tuesday.
         Sorry for you.
Hope, though, since then, some fair maid has con-
    soled you?

No? Deuce you say. Poor fellow, that's too bad.
My wife—
       Of course I am! Hadn't I told you?
       I thought I had.

Ah, boys! These pleasant memories stealing o'er
    me—
I think I will take a Cabana now.
Thank you, old man. . . .
          You'll have to roll it for me—
       I forget how.

Well, this is pleasant. 'Bacco, tales vivacious,
  And beer. From youth's free spring once more I
    quaff,
A wild Bohemian.
         Five o'clock? Good—gracious!
       So much? I'm off!

No, positively can't. My wife—my dinner.
  Always in, evenings; people sometimes call.
(Here, Jack! one word—no grudge against the
    winner?
      Shake!)
       Good-bye, all!

And—I suppose my small domestic heaven
   Wouldn't much interest you? If it did—
Fellows! come up next Sunday—tea at seven—
      And . . . .
                    see . . . .
                           my kid.
         [*Quick Curtain.*]

As these specimens of his stanzas indicate, the editor of *Puck* contributed to its columns verses of various kinds, sometimes broadly comic, sometimes delicately playful. His range included "comic copy" neatly rhymed and also the more fanciful *vers de société*. As an example of this more difficult variety may be taken the sequence of couplets which he called 'Interesting':

I rowed her out on the broad bright sea,
Till the land lay purple upon our lee.

The heavens were trying the waves to outshine,
With never a cloud to the far sea-line.

On the reefs the billows in kisses broke—
But oh, I was dying for one small smoke.

She spoke of the gulls and the waters green—
But what is nature to Nicotine?

She spoke of the tides, and the Triton myth;
And said Jones was engaged to the blonde Miss
    Smith.

She spoke of her liking lemon on clams;
And Euclid, and parallelograms.

For her face was fair and her eyes were brown,
And she was a girl from Boston town.

And I rowed and thought—but I never said—
"Does Havana tobacco trouble your head?"

She talked of algæ—she talked of sand—
And I thought: "Tobacco you cannot stand."

She talked of the ocean-steamers' speed—
And I yearned for a whiff of the wicked weed.

And at last I spoke, between fright and fret:
"Would you mind if I smoked a cigarette?"

She dropped her eyes on the ocean's blue,
And said: "Would you mind if *I* smoked too?"

Not all of his *vers de société* were contributed to *Puck;* many of them were published by the *Century,* which was then
known as *Scribner's Monthly.* Among
these was one poem which "went the rounds

of the papers" when it first appeared, but which has since dropped out of sight, since its author refrained from reprinting it; 'In a Paris Restaurant':

I gaze, while thrills my heart with patriot pride,
  Upon the exquisite skin, rose-flushed and creamy;
The perfect little head; on either side
  Blonde waves. The dark eyes, vaguely soft and
    dreamy,
Hold for a space my judgment in eclipse,
  Until with half a pout, supremely dainty,
"He's real mean"—slips from out the strawberry
  lips—
          "Oh, ain't he?"

This *at* her escort, youthful, black-moustached
  And diamond-studded—this reproof, whereat he
Is not to any great extent abashed.
  (That youth's from "Noo Orleens" or "Cincin-
    natty,"
I'm sure.) But she—those dark eyes doubtful
  strike
  Her sherbet-ice . . . . Won't touch it. . . . Is in-
    duced to.
Result: "I'd sooner eat Mince-Pie, Jim, *like*
          We used to."

While then my too-soon-smitten soul recants,
  I hear her friend discoursing with much feeling

Of tailors, and a garment he calls "pants."
  I note into her eyes a softness stealing—
A shade of thought upon her low, sweet brow—
  She hears him not—I swear, I could have cried
    here—
The escort nudges her—she starts, and—"How?
    The *i*deer !"

This was the finishing and final touch.
  I rose, and took no further observation.
·I love my country "just about" as much—
  I have for it as high a veneration—
As a man whose fathers fought for liberty,
  Whose veins conduct the blood of Commodore
    Perry, can.
But *she* was quite too very awfully
    American.

To this magazine was also contributed a group of poems in the fixed forms which the younger versifiers of that day had just imported from France *via* England. The pathetic little triolet on a 'Pitcher of Mignonette,' the rondels 'She was a Beauty' and 'Ready for the Ride,' a rondeau or two, he preserved in his first volume of verse; but the most daring of them all, a triumphant chant-royal, always seemed to

him to be too broadly humorous to be
worthy of inclusion among his other poems,
and yet in no other chant-royal in English
have the difficulties of the form been more
ingeniously or more successfully overcome.
He gave it a flambuoyant title, 'Behold the
Deeds':

*[Being the Plaint of Adolphe Culpepper Ferguson,
Salesman of Fancy Notions, held in durance of his
Landlady for a "failure to connect" on Saturday
night.]*

I.

I would that all men my hard case might know,
  How grievously I suffer for no sin:
I, Adolphe Culpepper Ferguson, for lo!
  I of my landlady am lockéd in,
For being short on this sad Saturday,
Nor having shekels of silver wherewith to pay:
  She has turned and is departed with my key;
  Wherefore, not even as other boarders free,
    I sing (as prisoners to their dungeon-stones
  When for ten days they expiate a spree);
    Behold the deeds that are done of Mrs. Jones!

II.

One night and one day have I wept my woe;
  Nor wot I, when the morrow doth begin,

If I shall have to write to Briggs & Co.,
    To pray them to advance the requisite tin
For ransom of their salesman, that he may
Go forth as other boarders go alway—
    As those I hear now flocking from their tea,
Led by the daughter of my landlady
    Piano-ward. This day, for all my moans,
Dry bread and water have been servéd me.
    Behold the deeds that are done' of Mrs. Jones!

III.

Miss Amabel Jones is musical, and so
    The heart of the young he-boardèr doth win,
Playing "The Maiden's Prayer," *adagio*—
    That fetcheth him, as fetcheth the "bunko skin"
The innocent rustic. For my part, I pray:
That Badarjewska maid may wait for aye
    Ere sits she with a lover, as did we
Once sit together, Amabel! Can it be
    That all that arduous wooing not atones
For Saturday shortness of trade dollars three?
    Behold the deeds that are done of Mrs. Jones!

IV.

Yea! she forgets the arm that was wont to go
    Around her waist. She wears a buckle, whose
    pin
Galleth the crook of the young man's elbów.
    I forget not, for I that youth have been.
Smith was aforetime the Lothario gay.
Yet once, I mind me, Smith was forced to stay

Close in his room. Not calm, as I, was he;
But his noise brought no pleasaunce, verily.
   Small ease he gat of playing on the bones
Or hammering on his stove-pipe, that I see.
   Behold the deeds that are done of Mrs. Jones!

V.

Thou, for whose fear the figurative crow
   I eat, accursed be thou and all thy kin!·
Thee will I show up—yea, up will I show
   Thy too thick buckwheats, and thy tea too thin.
Ay! here I dare thee, ready for the fray:
Thou dost *not* "keep a first-class house," I say!
   It dost not with the advertisements agree.
   Thou lodgest a Briton with a puggaree.
      And thou hast harbored Jacobses and Cohns,
Also a Mulligan. Thus denounce I thee!
   Behold the deeds that are done of Mrs. Jones!

ENVOY.

Boarders! the worst I have not told to ye:
She hath stolen my trousers, that I may not flee
   Privily by the window. Hence these groans.
There is no fleeing in a *robe de nuit*.
   Behold the deeds that are done of Mrs. Jones!

Bunner's literary executor, the friend
with whom he had written 'In Partnership' and to whom he had dedicated 'Airs

from Arcady,' made a choice from the
verses which had not been published when
the poet died and also from a brilliant
series of 'Ballads of the Town,' which had
been contributed from time to time, to the
pages of *Puck;* and these winnowed lyrics
were appended to the definitive edition of
Bunner's 'Poems,' a single volume which included both 'Airs from Arcady' and
'Rowen: Second-Crop Songs.' But none
of the poems, grave or gay, which the
author himself had seen fit to reject himself, were allowed to find a place in this
final volume, by which he will be judged
in the future. Yet these outcast verses
are not unworthy of their writer; and it
has seemed a pity to let them slip into the
swift oblivion of the back-number. They
may be rescued here, even though they
must not ever be included in the book
which bears the poet's own name. After
all, the author ought to have some rights,
and he ought to be able to pick and choose
those of his own writings by which he is

willing to be judged.   His feeling has been finely phrased by Mr. Aldrich:

Take what thou wilt, a lyric or a line,
    Take all, take nothing,—and God send thee cheer!
But my anathema on thee and thine
    If thou add'st aught to what is printed here!
    (1896).

XI

THE STRANGEST FEAT OF
MODERN MAGIC

IN the extremely interesting address of
Dr. Oliver Lodge, F.R.S., as president of the Society for Psychical
Research, which is printed in the
proceedings of the Society for March,
1902, there is a careful scientific consideration of various alleged occurrences which
seem to be contrary to the laws of nature as
we now understand them. Professor Lodge
discusses the proper attitude of a man of
science toward these alleged phenomena;
and he deplores the inveterate antagonism
between orthodox science and the accumu-
lating evidence that certain phenomena do
occur now and again which seem to be contrary to natural custom. He explains this
antagonism as due to the fact that "Science

has a horror of the unintelligible; it can make nothing of a capricious and disorderly agent, and it prefers to ignore the existence of any such."

But the attempt to ignore is in itself unscientific. It is the duty of Science to know —to know all that is to be known—and continually to extend the boundaries of knowledge, even though it is unable always to explain the immediate cause of every fact that it records.

Then Professor Lodge dismisses as unproved a host of alleged wonders of one kind or another, and he declares that full allowance must be made for "the ingenious and able impositions of a conjurer." He asserts that some of the psychical phenomena proclaimed to have occurred "bear a perilous resemblance to conjuring tricks," which can be very deceptive. He warns us that extreme caution is necessary, and full control must be allowed to the observers. He insists, moreover, that in so far as those professing to perform wonders demand their own conditions they must be content to be teated as conjurers.

There is one marvel wrought by the greatest of modern conjurers of which we have a true record, left us by the performer himself, who has told us what it was that he seemed to do, but who has not explained how he was able to accomplish the extraordinary feat. Robert-Houdin was the creator of the latter-day methods of modern magic; he was the inventor of many of the most ingenious and novel illusions, including the intricate and puzzling exhibition known as "second-sight." He defined himself as "a comedian playing the character of a magician." Late in life he wrote an account of his many adventures; and these "Confidences of a Prestidigitator" are worthy of comparison with all but the very best autobiographies—if not with Cellini's and Franklin's, at least with Cibber's and Goldoni's. Robert-Houdin's life of himself, quite as well as any of the others, would justify Longfellow's assertion that

RECREATIONS OF AN ANTHOLOGIST

"autobiography is what biography ought to be."

The special feat of Robert-Houdin's which has been mentioned was devised by him for exhibition in a palace and before a king—circumstances which exclude all suggestion of collusion or confederacy on the part of the audience. He tells us that in 1846 he was summoned to the Palace of Saint-Cloud to give a performance before Louis Philippe and the royal family. He had six days to make all his arrangements, and he invented one new trick for the occasion—a trick which could not possibly have been performed under any other circumstances. He tells us that early on the appointed morning a wagon from the royal stables came to fetch him (and his son, who assisted him), and to convey all his varied paraphernalia. A stage had been set up in one of the large saloons of the palace, the windows of which opened out on the broad and beautiful gardens, with their double rows of orange-trees, each growing in its square box on wheels. A sentry was placed at the door to see that the conjurer was not disturbed in his preparations. The King himself dropped in once to ask the entertainer if he had everything necessary.

At four o'clock in the afternoon, the King and the Queen, the members of the royal family, and a certain number of invited guests had assembled. The curtains were parted; and Robert-Houdin began to amuse and to puzzle his distinguished audience. He reserved for the end of his programme the so-called second-sight in which the son, blindfolded on the stage, named one after another all the objects which came into the father's hands, and even described them at length, giving the dates on coins and the inscriptions on watches. It was almost at the end of the programme, and just before the exhibition of second-sight, that Robert-Houdin accomplished the equally astonishing trick which he had invented for the occasion. In setting forth this feat we can follow his own accurate but summary account in the autobiography.

He began by borrowing half a dozen handkerchiefs from his noble spectators. These he took back to the stage and made into a package, which he left upon his table. Then he came down again among the audience with a pack of blank visiting-cards in his hand. He distributed these here and there among the spectators, requesting every one who received a card to write the name of a place where he or she would like the handkerchiefs to be conveyed instantly and invisibly. When a sufficient number of these cards had been written to insure a large variety of choice, Robert-Houdin gathered them up and went over to Louis Philippe.

The conjurer asked the King to pick out three cards and then to decide to which of the three places designated thereon he desired to have the handkerchiefs transported.

"Let us see," said the monarch, as he looked at the first card he had taken. Then he read, "I desire that the handkerchiefs should be found under one of the candelabra on the chimney." The King looked up and said, "That is too easy for a sorcerer." So he read the writing on the second card, "that the handkerchiefs should be carried to the dome of the Invalides." With his customary shrewdness the King commented on this, saying that it might suit if it was not a great deal too far away, "not for the handkerchiefs—but for us."

Finally, Louis Philippe glanced at the third card, which he did not read aloud at once, as he had read the others.

"Ah, ha!" he said, "I'm rather afraid that this would puzzle you! Do you know what it proposes?"

"Will your majesty be kind enough to inform me?" answered Robert-Houdin.

"This card," answered the monarch, "expresses the wish that you should cause the handkerchiefs to pass inside the box in which an orange-tree is growing, the last one on the right."

Robert-Houdin answered, promptly, "Is that all, Sire? Give the order and I will obey."

"So be it," Louis Philippe responded; "I shall not be sorry to see a deed of magic. So I choose the box of the orange-tree."

Then the King whispered an order or two, and several persons ran out promptly into the garden and stationed themselves about the orange-tree—"guarding against any fraud," as Robert-Houdin himself puts it.

The magician went back on the stage, and, putting the package of handkerchiefs on the centre of his table, he covered it with a ground-glass bowl. Then, taking his wand, he tapped on the bowl and bade the handkerchiefs begone to their appointed place. When he lifted the glass the little package had disappeared; and in its stead there was a white turtle-dove with a ribbon about its neck.

At this moment the King went swiftly to the glass door, through which he could see out into the garden; he wanted to make sure that his messengers were keeping faithful guard over the orange-tree.

Turning to the conjurer with an ironic smile, he said: "Ah, *Monsieur le Sorcier,* I'm doubtful about the virtue of your magic wand!"

Then the King gave orders to call the master-gardener and to tell him to open the box of the orange-tree at the end of the row on the right.

The master-gardener came immediately; and although greatly astonished at the order, he began work at once on the front of the box. Soon he had removed one of the upright panels of which it was composed.

Apparently he found the soil undisturbed, as he inserted his hand carefully in among the roots of the growing tree without discovering anything.

Suddenly a cry of surprise broke from him; and he withdrew his hand, holding a small iron casket eaten with rust.

This strange treasure-trove, scraped clean of the soil that incrusted it, was brought in and placed on a little table near the King.

"Well, monsieur," cried Louis Philippe, with a movement of impatient curiosity, "here's a box. Are the handkerchiefs contained in that, by some strange chance?"

"Yes, Sire," the conjurer replied, with assurance. "They are there—and they have been there for a very long while!"

"A long while?" returned the monarch; "how can that be, as it is not a quarter of an hour since the handkerchiefs were given to you?"

"I cannot deny that, Sire," responded the magician; "but where would the magic be if I could not accomplish things absolutely incomprehensible? No doubt, your majesty will be even more surprised when I prove beyond all question that this casket and what it contains were deposited in the box of the orange-tree sixty years ago!"

"I should like to be able to take your word for it," said the King, smiling; "but really I cannot do that. In a case like this I shall insist on proof."

"If your majesty will only open the iron casket," returned the conjurer, "you will find therein abundant proof of what I have asserted."

"Before I can open the casket, I must have the key," objected the monarch.

"You can have the key, Sire, whenever you please," explained the magician. "You have only to detach it from the neck of the turtle-dove."

Louis Philippe untied the ribbon which was around the neck of the bird, and which held a little rusty key. With this the King hastily opened the casket.

The first object that presented itself to the eyes of the monarch was a parchment. He took it up and opened it. This is what he read:

"*To-day, June 6, 1786.*
"*This iron box, containing six handker-chiefs, was placed within the roots of an*

orange-tree by me, Balsamo, Count Cagli-
ostro, to be used in the accomplishing of an
act of magic, which shall be performed
sixty years from to-day, before Louis Phi-
lippe and his family."

"Decidedly," remarked the monarch, now even more astonished, "this smacks of witchcraft. Nothing is lacking, since both the signature and seal of the celebrated sorcerer are here at the bottom of this document, which, God forgive me, seems to smell of sulphur."

To this gracious pleasantry of the sovereign the courtiers paid the proper tribute of laughter.

Then the King took from out the box a carefully sealed package of parchment.

"Is it possible," he asked, "that the handkerchiefs are wrapped in this?"

"Indeed, Sire, that is where they are," answered Robert-Houdin. "But before opening I beg that your majesty will note that the package is also sealed with the seal of Count Cagliostro."

"Certainly," said the monarch, looking twice at the red wax with its firm impression. "It is the same."

And immediately the King, impatient to discover the contents of the packet, tore it open, and spread out before the spectators the six handkerchiefs which the conjurer had borrowed only a few minutes earlier.

This is the account Robert-Houdin himself gives; and it may be well to record that he always bore the reputation of being a truthful man. Nothing more extraordinary was ever performed by any mere conjurer; indeed, this feat is quite as startling as any of those attributed to Cagliostro himself, and it has the advantage of being accurately and precisely narrated by the inventor. Not only is the thing done a seeming impossibility, but it stands forth the more impressively because of the spectacular circumstances of its performance—a stately palace, a lovely garden, the assembled courtiers and the royal family. The magician had to depend on his wits alone, for he was deprived of all the advantages of his own theatre and of all possibility of aid from a confederate mingled amid the casual spectators.

Robert-Houdin was justified in the gentle pride with which he told how he had thus astonished the King of the French. He refrained from any explanation of the means whereby he wrought his mystery, believing that what is unknown is ever the more magnificent. He did no more than drop a hint or two, telling the reader that he had long possessed a cast of Cagliostro's seal, and suggesting slyly that when the King sent messengers out into the garden to stand guard over the orange-tree the trick was already done, and all precautions were then futile.

Yet, although the inventor·chose to keep his secret, any one who has mastered the principles of the art of magic can venture an explanation. Robert-Houdin has set forth the facts honestly; and with the facts solidly established it is possible to reason out the method employed to accomplish a deed which, at first sight, seems not only impossible but incomprehensible.

The first point to be emphasized is that Robert-Houdin was as dexterous as he was ingenious. He was truly a prestidigitator, capable of any sleight-of-hand. Nothing was simpler for so accomplished a performer than the substitution of one package for another, right before the eyes of all the spectators. And it is to be remembered that although the palace was the King's the apparatus on the extemporized stage was the magician's. Therefore, when he borrowed six handkerchiefs and went up on the stage and made them up into a package, which remained on a table in sight of everybody, we can grant without difficulty that the package which remained in sight did not then contain the borrowed handkerchiefs.

In fact, we may be sure that the borrowed handkerchiefs had been conveyed somehow to Robert-Houdin's son, who acted as his assistant. When the handkerchiefs were once in the possession of the son out of sight behind the scenery or hangings of the stage, the father would pick up his pack of blank visiting-cards and distribute a dozen of them or a score, moving to and fro in very leisurely fashion, perhaps going back to the stage to get pencils, which he would also give out as slowly as possible, filling up the time with playful pleasantry, until he should again catch sight of his son. Then, and not until then, would he feel at liberty to collect the cards and take them over to the King.

When the son had got possession of the handkerchiefs, he would smooth them swiftly, possibly even ironing them into their folds. Then he would put them into the parchment packet, which he would seal twice with Cagliostro's seal. Laying them in the bottom of the rusty iron casket, he would put on top the other parchment, which had already been prepared, with its adroit imitation of Cagliostro's handwriting. Snapping down the lid of the casket, the lad would slip out into the corridor and steal into the garden, going straight to the box of the appointed orange-tree. He could do this unobserved, because no one was· then suspecting him, and because all the spectators were then engaged in thinking up odd places to which the handkerchiefs might be transported. Already, in the long morning, probably while the royal household was at its midday breakfast, the father or the son had loosened one of the staples in the back of the box in which the designated orange-tree was growing. The lad now removed this staple and thrust the casket into the already-prepared hole in the centre of the roots of the tree. Then he replaced the staple at the back of the box, feeling certain that whoever should open the box in front would find the soil undisturbed. This most difficult part of the task once accomplished, he returned to the stage, or at least in some way he signified to his father that he had accomplished his share of the wonder, in the performance of which he was not supposed to have any part.

On seeing his son, or on receiving the signal that his son had returned, Robert-Houdin would feel himself at liberty to collect the cards on which various spectators had written the destinations they proposed for the package of handkerchiefs, which was still in full sight. He gathered up the cards he had distributed; but as he went toward the King he substituted for those written by the spectators others previously prepared by himself—a feat of sleight-of-hand quite within the reach of any ordinary performer. Of these cards, prepared by himself, he forced three on the sovereign;—and the forcing of cards upon a kindly monarch would present little difficulty to a prestidigitator of Robert-Houdin's consummate skill.

When the three cards were once in the King's hands, the trick was done, for Robert-Houdin knew Louis Philippe to be a shrewd man in small matters. Therefore, it

226

was reasonably certain that when the King had to make a choice out of three places, one near and easy, a second remote and difficult, and a third both near and difficult, Louis Philippe would surely select the third, which was conveniently at hand, and which seemed to be at least as impossible as either of the others.

The event proved that the conjurer's analysis of the King's character was accurate; yet one may venture the opinion that the magician had taken every needed precaution to avoid failure, even if the monarch had made another selection. Probably Robert-Houdin had one little parchment packet hidden in advance somewhere in the dome of the Invalides and another tucked up out of sight in the base of one of the candelabra on the chimney-piece; and if either of the other destinations had been chosen, the substitute packet would have been produced, and the magician would then have offered to transport it also into the box of the orange-tree. And thus the startling climax of the marvel would have been only a little delayed.

When so strange a wonder can be wrought under such circumstances by means so simple, we cannot but feel the force of Dr. Lodge's warning that an unwavering scepticism ought to be the attitude of all honest investigators toward every one who professes to be able to suspend the operation of a custom of nature. No one of the feats attributed to Home, the celebrated medium who plied his trade in Paris during the Second Empire, was more abnormal than this trick of Robert-Houdin's, and no one of them is so well authenticated. It may be that certain of the customs of nature are not inexorable, and that we shall be able to discover exceptions now and again. But the proof of any alleged exception, the evidence in favor of any alleged violation of the custom of nature, ought to be overwhelming.

(1902).

THE END.